# PRAISE FOR
# SET YOURSELF FREE IN RELATIONSHIPS

*Shirley Smith's work is brilliantly evolutionary. This book shows you the way to authentic power in your relationships.*
Paul & Layne Cutright, Authors of the best selling<br>'You're Never Upset for the Reason You Think'

*My wife and I sought Shirley Smith's help in healing our dysfunctional relationship. Her program as described in* **Set Yourself Free in Relationships** *takes an holistic approach by empowering ourselves to deal with the underlying causes that brought our relationships to crisis point. We strongly endorse her approach as it has worked miracles for us.*
Ian & Miriam Golding

*Before doing the work presented in this book I did not know how to ask for what I wanted in a relationship. I didn't even know what I really wanted! I created my present from my past and I was confused and angry within my marriage. Now, with my past definitely where it belongs, I relate from a place of clarity, choice and confidence. I am choosing and creating nurturing, exciting and healthy relationships in my life that support me to develop spiritually, emotionally and intellectually.*
Paula Forrest, Actor, Mother, Teacher

*When it comes to matters of the heart, this book gets right to the heart of the matter. Highly recommended reading.*
John Stellios, MD

*My husband and I committed to working through* **Set Yourself Free in Relationships** *together as we navigated a rocky period in our 21 year relationship.*

*We are now experiencing greater togetherness, understanding and ultimately an intimacy that neither of us thought possible. The most wonderful change for me personally is I now know myself better as well as have a partner I can share my fears, hopes and desires with, one who understands my need to talk about my feelings.*

E. M., Coach & Psychotherapist

*The skills in this book saved my relationship...I only wish I had read it years ago.*

Bill Dowzer, Architect

*Having completed the exercises featured in this book, gave us a wonderful insight on human behavior and how to communicate effectively to meet our own needs within a relationship. To participate in doing family of origin work, with our family, was the best inheritance that we could give to our children. The knowledge that we have gained from this unique work that Shirley does, is the key to successful relationships, personal freedom and to achieve the very best in our lives. We highly recommend for anyone to read* **Set Yourself Free in Relationships.**

Tony & Glenda Rowett, Farmers/Horticulture

**Set Yourself Free in Relationships** *shows us how to become an individual in the chaos of relationships. With this information we discover where we end and others begin and the relationship becomes a channel for growth rather than a cause of overwhelming hopelessness.*

Geoffrey Carthy, Counselor/Psychotherapist - Hobart, Australia

## ABOUT THE AUTHOR

Shirley Smith, Managing Director of the Radiant Group Pty Ltd, is a human behavior expert, a highly recognized presenter and the author of two best selling books, *Set Yourself Free, The Game of Life Playbook* and now her third book, *Set Yourself Free in Relationships*. With degrees in philosophy; divinity; a background in psychology and behavioral science, Shirley draws on 20 years experience in human functioning to help people identify and change behavior patterns which block success and disrupt relationships. A firm believer in getting the most out of life, Shirley coaches people to design life strategies that enrich relationships, ensure success and let them enjoy their lives. Her style is 'down to earth' and 'tell-it-like-it-is'.

Originally from the USA, Shirley was brought to Australia 17 years ago to train psychologists, doctors, counselors and health professionals in the treatment of co-dependency, addictive behavior and family of origin issues. Not only is Shirley recognized as one of Australia's leading specialists in this field, she is also a Certified Trainer and Facilitator in the educational applications of Neuro-Linguistic Programming and Generative Learning. In addition, Shirley is a certified hypnotist and an accredited Myers Briggs practitioner.

Shirley's work has been featured in nearly every mainstream Australian publication. As *New Woman* magazine's choice of Executive Coach, Shirley wrote a monthly column for their readers and has appeared on a number of television shows, as well as being featured on talkback radio programs Australia-wide.

After moving to Australia in 1988, Shirley became an Australian citizen in 1994, making her home in Sydney's North Shore and the Blue Mountains with her husband Eric. She loves theatre, film, dance, new adventures and enjoys spending time with good friends and playing with her little dog, "Sassy".

For further information; to book an executive coaching session; a keynote address; enroll in one of The Radiant Group's Programs, Events or Seminars; or to contact Shirley Smith:

The Radiant Group Pty. Ltd.
PO Box 1605, Neutral Bay NSW Australia, 2089
Tel: 61 (0)2 9953 7000
Fax: 61 (0)2 9953 7100
E-mail: info@theradiantgroup.com.au
Website: www.theradiantgroup.com.au
or www.shirleysmith.com

**Set Yourself Free in Relationships**
*Essential Skills to teach others how to treat you*

Published by:
Artisan Educational Systems, LLC, Nevada, USA
info@theradiantgroup.com.au
Copyright © Shirley Smith 2005

Distributed in Australia by
Brumby Books Pty Ltd
10 Southfork Drive
Kilsythe South
Victoria 3137
Phone: +61 3 9761 5535
www.brumbybooks.com.au

All rights reserved. No part of this publication may be reproduced, stored in a retrieval system or transmitted in any form or by any means, electronic, mechanical, photocopying, recording or otherwise, without the prior permission of the publishers.

**Set Yourself Free in Relationships** - *Essential skills to teach others how to treat you.*
ISBN 0-9772760-0-7

Cover Design: Dolores Knox - Union Street Studio Pty Ltd
Layout and Design: Dolores Knox - Union Street Studio Pty Ltd
Photography: Cornish Photography
Printed in Australia by Griffin Pty Ltd

# SET YOURSELF FREE
## *in Relationships*

**ESSENTIAL SKILLS
TO TEACH
OTHERS HOW TO
TREAT YOU**

## SHIRLEY SMITH

# DEDICATION

I dedicate this book
to my darling husband,
Eric Rose,
the best man I know.

# CONTENTS

FOREWORD .................................................................... I

ACKNOWLEDGEMENTS ........................................... V

INTRODUCTION: DANCING WITH DADDY ............ VII

**CHAPTER 1: YOU - ME - WE** .......................................... 1
**Identity is the basic distinction of self: who am I?** ............... 1
Diagram 1: Three Separate Identities .................................... 2
**Is it intimacy or is it intensity?** ............................................ 2
**Give your relationships a health check-up** ......................... 4
Diagram 2: Healthy Relationship Model ............................... 5
Diagram 3: Unhealthy Relationship Model ........................... 6
**Repairing and strengthening your personal foundation** ..... 7
**Needs, values, wants and desires** ....................................... 8
Needs .................................................................................... 9
Values .................................................................................. 10
Wants ................................................................................... 11
Desires ................................................................................. 12
Diagram 4: Needs, Values, Wants, Desires ......................... 13
**Identifying dependent relationships** ................................. 14
Characteristics of polarized, unhealthy dependency ........... 15

Examples of unhealthy, dependent attitudes and behavior..........16
**Pinpointing your 'payoffs'**..................................................19
**The Pandora paradox**.......................................................22
**Accountable action**..........................................................24
Exercise 1: Observing relationship patterns.........................24
Exercise 2: Assessing your unmet needs..............................26
Exercise 3: Facing and embracing your neediness and needlessness. 28

**CHAPTER 2: ANCHORS AWAY**..................................31
**Familiar or family?**...........................................................32
Diagram 5: Family Roles...................................................33
**Beliefs**............................................................................36
Limiting beliefs.................................................................37
**Feelings**..........................................................................38
Adult feelings...................................................................39
Carried feelings.................................................................39
Adult-to-adult feeling exchange.........................................40
Unresolved childhood feelings...........................................42
**Behaviors**........................................................................43
The missing link...............................................................45
**Good Grief!**....................................................................48
Self-care while healing unresolved grief..............................50
**Accountable action**..........................................................52
Exercise 4: Intimacy - values - family roles.........................52
Exercise 5: Assessing your feelings.....................................54
Exercise 6: Assessing your beliefs.......................................55
Exercise 7: Assessing your behaviors..................................56
Exercise 8: Breaking patterns.............................................57

**CHAPTER 3: THE ROMANCE TRANCE**......................59
Whenever our identity is disrupted or destablized...............60
Trauma............................................................................61
Life changes and development transitions..........................61
Intentional trance.............................................................61
**Are you swinging or dancing between polarities?**.............61
Diagram 6: Swinging in Polarities.....................................63

Diagram 7: Dancing between the Polarities..................63
**Mary's Story**..................64
**Co-addicted Relationships**..................68
**What is love?**..................70
**You might as well face it - you're addicted to love**..................72
The Co-addictive Love Dance..................74
Diagram 8: Co-addictive Love Dance..................76
Enmeshment..................77
Escapes from intimacy..................77
Romance addiction..................78
Sex addiction..................81
Relationship addiction..................84
Are you in ritual or are you in relationship?..................85
**To open a new door…close the old one**..................86
**Treating co-addictive relationships**..................88
Stages of withdrawal..................90
**Accountable action**..................92
Exercise 9: Completing relationships process..................92
Exercise 10: Treatment for co-addicted relationships..................95
Exercise 11: Keys to interdependency..................98

**CHAPTER 4: BREAKING THE FANTASY BOND**..................101
**Abandonment: the root of dependency**..................103
Physical abandonment..................104
Abandonment through abuse..................105
Emotional abandonment..................105
**The Fantasy Bond**..................108
Hunger vs. Love..................109
Effects on intimate relationships..................111
Idealized parent: the voice and the mystical image..................112
**Grief: the key to healing abandonment**..................115
Enough time..................116
Validation..................116
Non-shaming support..................117
**Accountable action**..................119
Exercise 12: Embracing abandonment and engulfment..................120

Exercise 13: Mystical image of your ideal partner ...................... 125
Diagram 9: Mystical Image ............................................................ 127
Exercise 14: Writing a fairytale of your childhood ...................... 128

**CHAPTER 5: CREATING INTIMACY** ................................... 131
**Into Me I C** ................................................................................ 132
**Boundaries** ................................................................................ 135
**Standards** .................................................................................. 136
**Characteristics of intimacy in a relationship** ......................... 136
**Obstacles to intimacy** ............................................................... 138
**Boundaries: the key to teaching others how to treat you** ........ 139
Types of boundaries .................................................................... 142
**Guidelines for couples remaining in a relationship** ................ 144
**The five stages of partnership** ................................................. 146
1. Attraction ................................................................................ 147
2. Power struggle ........................................................................ 147
3. Co-operation ........................................................................... 147
4. Synergy .................................................................................... 147
5. Completion ............................................................................. 148
**Seven steps to building healthy relationships** ......................... 150
**Active accountability** ............................................................... 154
Exercise 15: Meeting your needs in relationships ...................... 157
Exercise 16: How to set boundaries ............................................ 166
Exercise 17: Intimacy-building questions for
romantic relationships ................................................................ 168
Exercise 18: Creating an Intimate Relationship ......................... 172
Diagram 10: Current Relationship .............................................. 174
Diagram 11: Analysis of Current Relationship .......................... 178
Diagram 12: Future Relationship ................................................ 181

**EPILOGUE: THE LAST DANCE** ........................................... 183

**BIBLIOGRAPHY AND SUGGESTED READING** ................ 187

# FOREWORD

One of our greatest challenges as human beings is to foster healthy relationships. Relating to your own self in a healthy, mature way is vital to healthy relating with other people, and provides a foundation for spiritual growth and evolution.

For the past fourteen years I have been working as a medical practitioner. My primary focus has been on the physical body and its ailments. Currently, I practice as an anaesthesiologist, sub-specializing in cardiothoracic anaesthesiology and medical perfusion. As a medical practitioner I assist unconscious people undergoing surgery, while as a counselor, I facilitate people out of their anaesthetised, numb state into a conscious life with feeling and connection to their true self.

The human heart has always held a fascination for me, its strength and power and its vulnerability to illness. I am now able to see the human heart as more than just an organ. I appreciate its despair when shut down and its power to love when it is open. I, too, have felt this on my personal journey as I have moved towards finding the unique strength of my own heart.

Relationships are part of our emotional food and nourishment. The dynamics of relationships may at times be confusing and disheartening. Being caught in the spiral of unhealthy relating can make you ill - physically, emotionally, psychologically, sexually, spiritually and may even prove life threatening. There are various ways that unhealthy patterns appear in our lives, such as addictions, depression, high separation rates, domestic violence and sexual abuse.

The symptoms of dysfunctional relating can also be passed down to future generations. Left untreated, they may prevent you from evolving and maturing and leave you feeling stuck, miserable, numb, hurt and unhappy.

Shirley Smith's dedication to this field for over twenty years has given her an enormous amount of experience in human functioning. My personal and professional involvement with Shirley has shown me the positive influence and clarity of her work. It has also demonstrated to me the power of dysfunctional relating and its negative effects on individuals, families and society.

Shirley's creativity and passion have made this book possible. She presents information in a clear, concise and easy-to-read way to appeal to everyone. It is her commitment to her own growth and to that of her clients that is a mark of her integrity and pioneering spirit.

*Set Yourself Free in Relationships* provides you with a powerful resource, which involves education, exercises, a guide for finding emotional support and validation. It also demonstrates a framework for healthy, deep grieving and healing. The book details examples of common issues and struggles within relationships, including how to work towards solutions. As a result you will be able to teach others to treat you in the healthy way you deserve. This may mean being acknowledged or loved, or not accepting the abusive behavior of other people. If rewarding and enriched relationships are what you are seeking, then there *is* hope!

I strongly recommend that you read and complete the exercises in this book as well as find the support that you need. Shirley's work has been the catalyst for enormous growth in my own life and many others to which I have had the honor to bear witness. Being accountable for our own selves is the first step to freedom from living in the past and opening the door to the life you deserve.

I sincerely hope that your journey is full of adventure, passion for your deepest desires and the fulfilment of rich, rewarding relationships that really open your heart. The answers to your relationship issues are already within you. The power to change your relationships is now in your hands.

With love and heartfelt compassion,
*Dr John Stellios M.D.*

# ACKNOWLEDGEMENTS

*"As an individual your power is limited.
When you join with others, it becomes unlimited."*

The Story Teller

No one writes a book alone. This book is about relationships - and it is because of many wonderful relationships that this book is in your hands. I especially want to thank and acknowledge the people who have joined with me in this adventure.

Firstly, I want to thank the many clients I've worked with on relationship issues over the years. Your courage, honesty and willingness to transform your relationships continue to inspire me.

I am grateful to the pioneering teachers whose contribution to my life and my work is rippling to you through this book. They are Terry Cole-Whittaker, Yah Weh, Robert Firestone, Milton Erickson, John Bradshaw, Pia Mellody and Anne Wilson Schaef.

A heart felt thanks to those who have personally supported me. Eric Rose, my dance partner in life, thanks for cooking for me, loving me and mostly for putting up with me while writing this book. My late father, John Smith and my mother Laura Smith for loving me no matter what and doing the best they could. My dear friend, Cherie Kellahan, for believing in me, supporting me and giving valuable feedback on the manuscript. Dr John Stellios for careful consideration in writing the foreword to this book. My coach, Christine McDougall, for partnering with me and always telling me the truth. To my precious little companion Sassy, who patiently sat at my feet while I was writing, rather than going for a walk.

This book had a very tight deadline. I want to particularly thank the following people for their commitment to helping me meet it. To Natalie Rowett for her excellent feedback and input to the manuscript. Paul Cutright for his contribution to the cover, Siobhan Cantrill for burning the midnight oil to edit this book, Maurice Peters at Brumby Books for his insight and wisdom, and a special thank you to my designer, Dolores Knox who is not only extremely talented, but a joy to work with - and about to be a Mom any day.

Having a partner, who shares a vision and helps to create it, is one of the most rewarding experiences a person can have. I am especially fortunate and grateful to Nicole Helich for partnering with me on this book. Nicole has been involved in just about every aspect of this project. Her dedication and commitment to excellence has matched mine, making an impossible deadline possible. Thanks Nikki!

Finally, I thank God, the real reason this book is in your hands.

# INTRODUCTION

# DANCING WITH DADDY

Was my vision blurry from spinning round the dance floor or the tears spilling from my eyes? The polka music in my head had been on pause waiting for me to press the play button ever since my twelfth birthday, the first time my father asked me to dance with him. We were at Alpine Village, a German restaurant frequented by my Dad's side of the family. On that special day Daddy danced with me in front of all the relatives.

Dancing is an intimate experience. Connecting without words. Catching one's soul reflecting through their eyes. And if you're lucky, you let go, allowing the dance to take you to that special place where sensory-rich memories are programmed to stay with you forever.

Today, I wished I were twelve years old again. I pushed play and let myself drop into the memory.

My senses were flooded with pictures of my Dad, larger than life, his eyes dancing with laughter. I kept my eyes focused on his to stop me from being too dizzy. Feeling his strength guiding me, we spun round and round with the sounds of the 'Beer Barrel Polka' pounding in my chest. Daddy's feelings of pride suddenly transformed me into a princess - and I was having a ball!

My father and I danced many more times since that day.

Unfortunately, all of our dances weren't on the dance floor, nor were they pleasant.

Wiping my tears with my husband's handkerchief, we stood beside my father's hospital bed in the intensive care unit. Daddy had been in a coma for three weeks when we arrived from overseas. I watched my father, hanging on to life through tubes and needles. His eyes weren't dancing; they were closed. He wasn't laughing and he couldn't speak with the ventilator filling his throat.

My mother and sister had been waiting for me to arrive - to help them make *that* decision. It was clear that my father was suffering. Without life support, disease would have already overtaken him. Yet, my Mom just couldn't let him go. She told me on the phone that she needed more time. She wanted to talk with him, hold his hand, comb his hair and just be with him. Of course she needed more time to reach closure. My God, they'd been married for over 60 years. Just before we hung up, Mom promised to take him off life support when I got there. She wanted us to be together.

I stood on a footstool so I could put my cheek next to his. Stroking his forehead, I whispered in his ear, 'Daddy it's Shirley, I'm here to help you go home.' He opened his eyes and locked onto mine. I knew he had been waiting for me. Waiting to have our last dance.

I felt very grateful that I had resolved my past issues with my father and healed my childhood wounds from the relationship dynamics in our family. In that moment I knew with all of my heart that every bit of healing work I'd done in the past 20 years had been worth it. I was able to be 100 per cent present and intimately connect with my father to help him with this important transition. I didn't know it at the time, but I was about to receive the greatest gift my father had ever given me.

Although my Mom and Dad had been married for over 60 years, I wouldn't call their relationship happy or healthy. Void of intimacy and any real connection, they were welded at the hip, the 'Can't live with 'em and can't live without 'em' syndrome. Typically following their generation's norm, they played their roles well, my father appearing as the 'strong' one and my mother the 'weak one'.

Focusing on each other, especially each other's faults, my parents bickered constantly, each complaining about the other to my sister and me. I don't think they ever looked at their relationship or at themselves. Truthfully, they were caught in an 'addictive dance' that kept playing on and on like a broken record.

Paradoxically, in their 'Golden Years' my mother was the strong one - and boy did she resent it. Day after day they stayed at home, taking refuge from each other by moving from TV to TV in the oasis of the seven they owned. As the years went by, they seemed to move further apart.

For me the icing on the cake was watching my mother spend her final hours with my father in front of the TV in his hospital room. It was her time to say her final goodbye. From the corridor, I watched through a crack in the door. She said to him, 'It's TV time, Honey. Let's watch a movie.' He was in a coma! There was no connection, no final words of gratitude or love. How could this happen? How could a supposedly 'happy 60-year marriage' get so bad? When I looked at my husband witnessing this scene with tears in his eyes, I silently vowed that I would go to any lengths to maintain intimacy with him.

I don't mean to be critical of my parents. I know they tried to be happy as best they could. Living with untreated wounds from their childhood and lacking skills for healthy relating prevented my parents from enjoying intimacy and happiness together. And with the divorce rate over 50 per cent in the western world, my parents were in part of society's norm.

Although I didn't realize it at the time, I learned how to 'dance' in relationships from observing my mother and father when I was growing up. In fact, some of their worst relationship dynamics had

## INTRODUCTION

rented space in me! It's frightening when you find yourself repeating your parents' patterns in your relationships. I know this from 20 years of witnessing it in my clients. That shocking realization has been the wake-up call to learn to dance my own dance.

No one has to end up in a relationship like my parents. No one has to accept bad treatment, loneliness, dissatisfying relationships or a complete lack of connection. You have a choice - you really do.

Let me pause here and take off my 'daughter hat' and put on my 'professional hat'. For the past 20 years, my professional role has taken the form of minister, counselor, teacher, author, speaker, corporate trainer, executive coach and facilitator. Wearing these different hats has given me countless opportunities to witness and interact with just about every type of relationship dynamic you can imagine.

*What most of us don't realize (and my parents certainly didn't) is that we teach others how to treat us.*

My first book, *Set Yourself Free - a must-read for people caught in addictive behaviors and those who love them,* details how most people desiring freedom are really looking to escape situations. In order to be *free from* anything, you must first be free in it. Once you've achieved that, then you will find that you are *free to* clearly choose what you really want.

*Set Yourself Free* takes the reader on a spiritual journey to acquire personal freedom, reclaim their power and learn how to connect intimately with themselves. It shows the reader how to build a strong personal foundation so they can express themselves confidently, live a more balanced life and choose freely from their authentic self.

*Set Yourself Free in Relationships: Essential Skills to Teach Others How to Treat You,* will help you uncover and transform unhealthy dynamics of relating that cause you to recycle dissatisfying or destructive relationships. Typically these are fuelled with intensity, drama, covert manipulation and dependencies. These painful, soul-destroying dynamics are common in unhealthy relationships, and they evolve from unresolved issues in our formative years.

Relationships exist in this form because they serve a purpose. They effectively distract people from discovering their underlying issues (which are mostly subconscious) of loneliness, hurt, emptiness, resentment, rejection and the fear of intimacy.

Unless you heal these issues they'll be carried and replayed in current and future relationships - even future generations. The good news is, history doesn't have to repeat itself!

## HOW DO YOU KNOW IF YOU NEED TO SET YOURSELF FREE IN RELATIONSHIPS?

Consider the following questions:

1. Do you withhold love, affection, recognition, sex or money?
2. Are you staying in a relationship you know you should leave?
3. Do you keep quiet to avoid conflict?
4. Do you choose relationships or do they choose you?
5. Do you either lose yourself or feel engulfed in close relationships?
6. Are you unable to say 'No' without guilt or fear of rejection?
7. Do you end up hurting those you love the most?
8. Are you 'too busy' to establish or maintain good relationships?
9. Do your relationships lack lustre or do they feel empty?
10. Do people listen to you as much as you'd like?
11. Do you isolate yourself socially and emotionally?
12. Are you unable to confidently deal with difficult relationships without compromising your views or values?
13. Do you become needy as you get close to others?

14. Are you tired of being involved in relationships where you are 'walking on eggshells'?

15. Do you find negative family traits in your partner?

16. Do you swing between idealizing and crucifying your partner or other authority figures?

17. Do you have to be 'in control' of the relationship?

18. Do you overly fantasize about romantic relationships?

19. Are you becoming disillusioned about finding a partner?

20. Do you have difficulty maintaining or staying in a relationship?

**If you answered yes to any of the above - then reading this book and doing the exercises will completely transform the quality of your relationships.**

Setting yourself free in relationships requires one to be 'actively accountable'. Adopting this life-changing approach actually gives you the opportunity to have more control over your choices and to discover the higher purpose of your relationships. The three important characteristics of active accountability are:

## 1. CLARITY

It's been said many times, 'clarity leads to power.' First you need to clearly understand what you are doing or not doing that causes you to recycle disappointment, confusion, frustration, resentment, loneliness, hurt and which that is generated from your relationships or the lack of them.

You must then be able to identify and meet your own needs and stop throwing them into your relationships. Putting your needs into your relationships not only causes conflict, it keeps you confused. The confusion becomes a distraction and eventually takes you back into a destructive or addictive relationship pattern.

Once your needs are met, it is easier to identify what you really want and don't want. You participate with a purpose and intention in your relationships. By this I mean that you are clear about what benefits and pleasures *you will take* from a relationship and what *you will contribute* to a relationship.

## 2. HONESTY

Regarding relationships, honesty involves speaking your truth about how you feel, what you think and what you want without any intention to manipulate another. Withholding, avoiding, 'little white lies' and exaggerating are other forms of dishonesty.

The secret to resolving conflict is to first confront yourself internally. This means being clear on your thoughts, feelings and intent. Doing this effectively requires rigorous honesty. It is also important to honestly look at your behavior and the repetitive patterns or themes that surface in your relationships. What are you doing or not doing to keep them in place?

## 3. ABILITY TO DISCERN

To discern means to understand something that is not immediately obvious. Your ability to discern is critical if you want to have healthy interactions with others. This involves identifying what is your part and what is not; what you are accountable for and what you're not.

If you become upset with another, the key to discernment is again to check within yourself first. What are your limiting beliefs and the buried feelings that were triggered? Did any of your behavior contribute to the conflict? When you can be honest with what triggered your upset, then you can begin to discern what part of the conflict is yours and what is another's.

Reading this book will help you clear confusion so you know what you really want and so you can discern and be accountable for your part in interactions. The book also explains how to identify and meet your needs in relationships, which is a must for intimacy and healthy relating.

More importantly, *doing the exercises in this book* will relieve your pain and build your confidence. You will be able to close the door on past relationships that still haunt you. You will learn to create intimacy without losing yourself or feeling engulfed.

It's been said the hardest part of any journey is taking that first step.

In this case the first step is to set an intention to be free in your relationships and to grant that freedom to others. Once you commit to be *actively accountable,* you are well on your way to setting yourself free to have happy, healthy and satisfying relationships. The next chapter will give you an opportunity to begin.

I have a question for you before you begin: when it comes to your most important relationships, *who are you dancing with?*

Warmly,
Shirley Smith
October 2005

# CHAPTER 1

# YOU - ME - WE

They say opposites attract. I don't have statistics on this, yet many years of counseling people on relationship issues have proven this to me. The very opposing characteristics that fascinate one initially tend to be what frustrates one as the 'honeymoon phase' of the relationship ends and the real relating begins. This is where the problems start.

For couples to experience healthy relating there must be three identities. There is an identity of YOU, one of ME, and the relationship has its own separate identity - a WE. Problems arise from the inability to separate these three identities, which contributes to the YOU and ME getting tangled in dynamics of unskilled and unhealthy relating.

## IDENTITY IS THE BASIC DISTINCTION OF SELF: WHO AM I?

- Identity is the basis for organizing/navigating the self and the world.
- Identity is represented in many modalities: thoughts, feelings, histories, images and physical place.
- Identity is organized at multiple levels: world, culture, family, relationship, individual, intra-individual etc.

CHAPTER 1: YOU – ME – WE

- Identity is organic, dynamic and constructive (it needs to be recreated in an ongoing way).
- Identity has the dual function of preserving self (continuity) and changing self (discontinuity, growth).
- Identity moves through death/rebirth cycles.

The diagram below illustrates this clearly:

THREE SEPARATE IDENTITIES
DIAGRAM 1

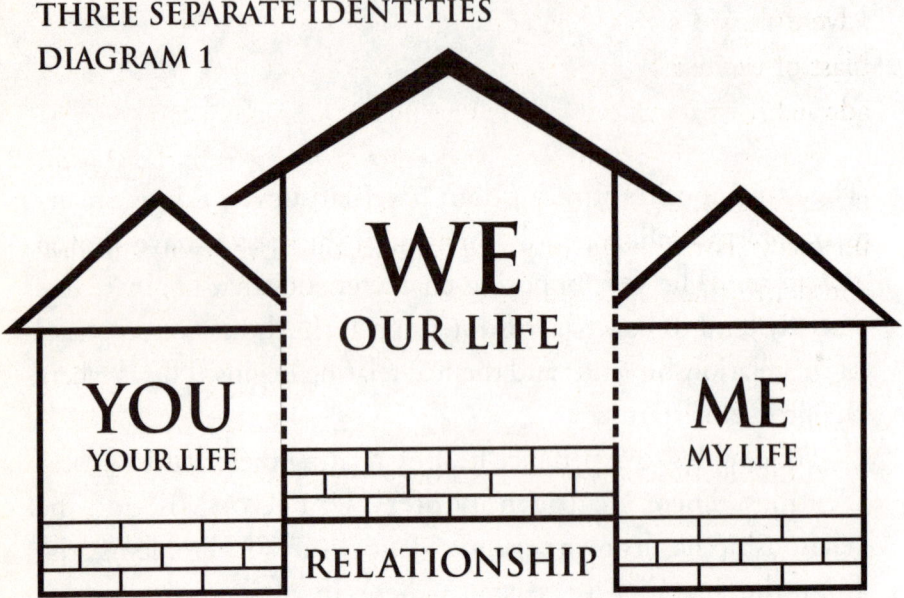

In this chapter I will show you models of healthy and unhealthy relationships (the WE), and the foundation of what you need to do to experience healthy relating (the YOU and ME).

## IS IT INTIMACY OR IS IT INTENSITY?

The greatest present you can give someone is to be present with him or her. I really understood the significant value of this after being with my father when he passed away. For my husband and I, the experience was completely void of intensity or drama and one of the most intimate times that we've shared with each other, as well as with my father.

The major reason people seek out counseling, buy books or enroll in personal development programs is to relieve pain from past unresolved relationships, mend problems in their current relationships and create more intimacy. What those seekers discover is that most people have intimacy confused with intensity.

Intimacy is like taking a cruise on the Caribbean and intensity is like racing in the America's Cup. Now before you categorize the cruise as boring, for the 'old folks' and the Cup for young adventurers, I suggest you bear in mind longevity. We all like a blast of excitement every now and then, but to live running on adrenalin wears us out and makes us old before our time.

From entertainment to advertisements, we are inundated with messages about sex and romance. After all, isn't that the basis of intimacy? Fortunately, intimate connections cover more breadth and depth than just sex and romance. Consider the following:

- Emotional intimacy: the food that sustains us and makes life yummy!

- Intellectual intimacy: exchanging stimulating information, ideas and possibilities.

- Physical intimacy: nurturing touch, hugs or someone to do something with.

- Spiritual intimacy: the joy of a great connection and the fulfillment it brings.

The 'connection' is what most people are after. Problem is, you can't have the connection with another until you have it with yourself first. If you want that connection, you have to be willing to share the most vulnerable and intimate parts of you - your personal, internal world - with a significant other, meaning your thoughts, feelings, wants, desires and what you value. To do this confidently, without the fear of rejection, is easier said than done.

Intensity in relationships is an addictive substitute for intimacy caused by unresolved childhood wounds such as neglect, abandonment, abuse, engulfment, extreme control and unmet childhood needs. Many are caught in an addictive cycle (a swirling dance) that is an intense replacement for true intimacy and real relating. This intensity *distracts* partners from discovering the real issue, acknowledging and dealing with the emptiness and loneliness in their relationship.

There is a simple, yet profound truth that's worth repeating. *'We teach people how to treat us.'* And most of what we teach, we do unconsciously. The secret to creating intimacy is to 'unlock' the unconscious patterns and repressed emotions causing one to recycle the same unfulfilling relationships. Once partners realize that the 'answer' to their relationship problems lie within, they then begin the journey that leads to healthy, happy relationships.

## GIVE YOUR RELATIONSHIPS A HEALTH CHECK-UP

So, what is healthy, anyway? The following models of healthy and unhealthy relationships are taken from what I've learned working with my clients over the past 20 years. They say 'a picture is worth a thousand words'. See if you recognize yourself or one of your relationships. I've used the analogy of building a house to show models of relationships.

## HEALTHY RELATIONSHIP MODEL
## DIAGRAM 2

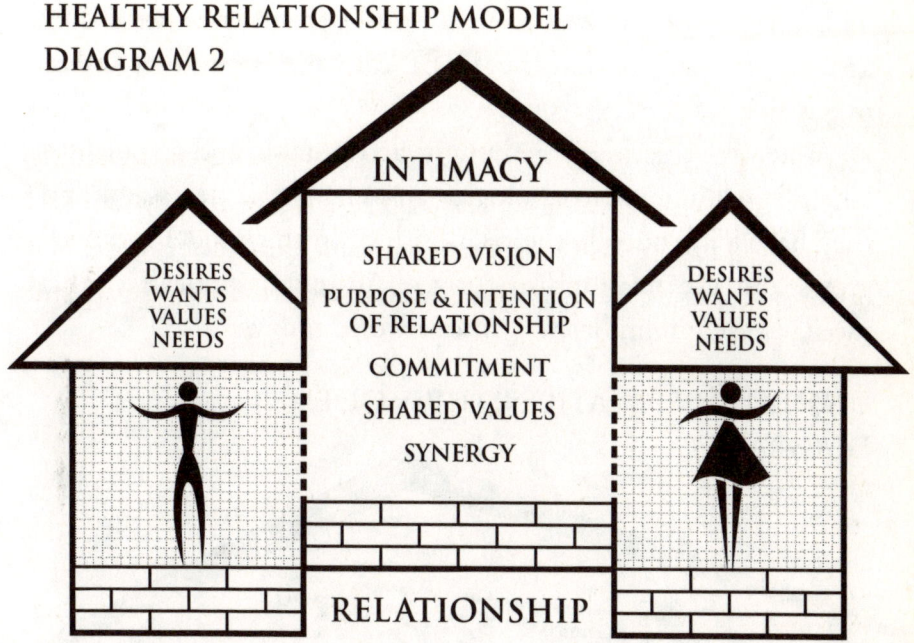

In this diagram there are two people standing side by side looking forward in the same direction, rather than at each other. This represents a shared vision. They stand outside the relationship, rather than being immersed, which lets them be objective.

They each have a solid personal foundation, meaning they have a good sense of self and a clear perspective of their values. Individually they are housed in a screened patio, representing personal boundaries. Rather than walls, boundaries are like screens. They let the air in and keep the bugs out. These two people know what they need, value, want and desire and, more importantly, they know how to meet their own needs.

They build an additional foundation for their relationship. Their relationship is a separate entity or in this case a house that they build together with separate needs wants and desires, as well as some shared values. It is their relationship that 'connects' them, providing the foundation for intimacy.

This couple lives in the questions, *'What can I contribute or give to the relationship?'* and *'What will I take from the relationship.'*

CHAPTER 1: YOU – ME – WE

This couple doesn't need to take from each other because they are solid individuals and they don't 'caretake' each other unless one is sick.

When relating, they are honest, accountable and responsive. There is willingness to apologize and change, if necessary, and they have a life outside the relationship. In this model intimacy grows and the relationship thrives. Although innovative, this model is the unfamiliar way in our world today.

## UNHEALTHY RELATIONSHIP MODEL
## DIAGRAM 3

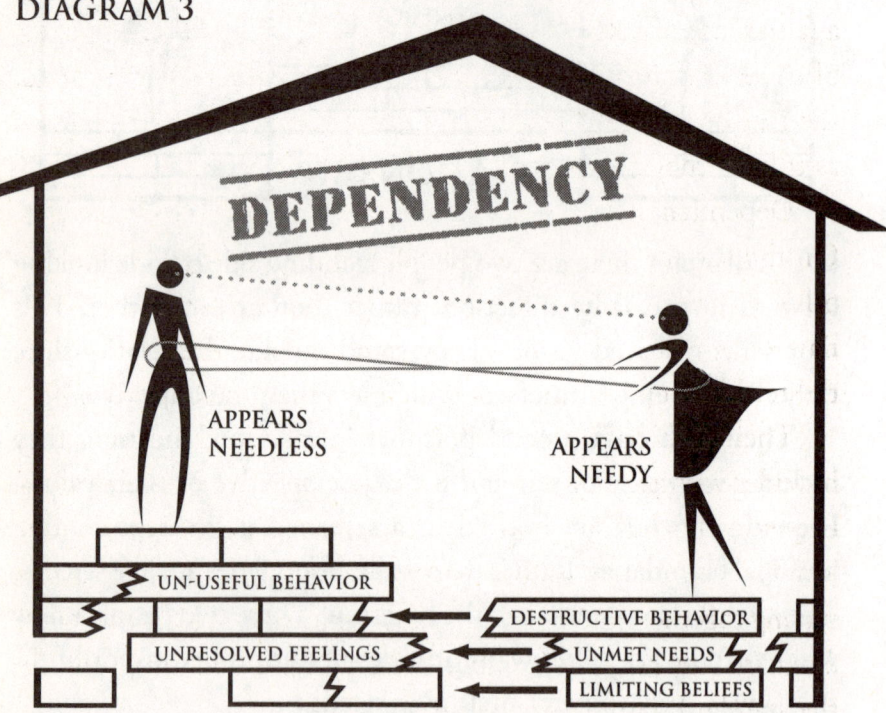

In this diagram the two people are inside the same house (no boundaries) and are facing each other. They are 'other focused' and enmeshed. To be enmeshed is to be entangled with someone that is difficult to separate from.

Look at their foundations. They can only stand strong by sliding together and using foundational components from the 'other' in relationship to what is missing in them. The foundation is faulty, with cracks and missing bricks, making the whole structure unstable, whether they are separate or apart. The faulty foundation represents unmet childhood needs and a false sense of value, which comes from their adapted childhood roles that they still act out as adults. Let me explain.

Children are needy by nature, not by choice. They instinctively adapt their behavior and personalities in order to get their emotional needs met. Children take on artificial roles to meet the deep psychological needs of the family, which gives the child a false sense of value. As the child grows, their false value grows, often leaving them with a lingering anxiety, a feeling of emptiness; the fear of being exposed as a fraud or complete bewilderment as to why they are misunderstood.

Dependency is the trademark of unhealthy relationships. On the surface, one person usually presents as needless and the other as needy. They are both needy and don't know it. They have an unconscious agenda to get their needs met either from the relationship or from each other.

Their relating is characterized by intensity, dishonesty (which includes withholding things) and a power struggle. They vacillate between being a persecutor, victim or rescuer. They manage to 'survive' the drama, and if you ask either of them why they are staying together, the response is, 'I love him/her.' This is the *'Can't live with 'em, can't live without 'em'* syndrome, and unfortunately, the standard, familiar model in our world today.

## REPAIRING AND STRENGTHENING YOUR PERSONAL FOUNDATION

As you can see, the reason so many of us have difficulties building healthy relationships is the lack of a strong and stable personal foundation.

Our personal foundation affects how we relate on all levels.

- **Physically** - behavioral patterns of relating. What behaviors are causing pain or frustration in your relationships?

- **Emotionally** - the most impaired level of relating because of buried feelings and insufficient education about how to handle emotions appropriately. Relationships are our emotional food. Are you stuffing or starving yourself?

- **Intellectually** - beliefs about yourself and others. Are negative or limited beliefs undermining your happiness?

- **Spiritually** - hope, trust, connection, intimacy. Are you feeling spiritually bankrupt in your relationships?

Relying on our relationships to meet our needs and form the foundation for our identity leads to chaos, confusion and never-ending misery. If we *take our value* (what we're worth) from our relationships, rather than *give value* to our relationships, we will perceive that we only have as much value as the relationship has. This is one of the reasons why people feel so awful when a relationship ends.

To create stable relationships and experience healthy relating, it is essential to have a strong personal foundation. It's equally important to understand the difference between needs, values, wants and desires and the vital part they play in relating.

## NEEDS, VALUES, WANTS AND DESIRES

Needs, values, wants and desires are the core components of a personal foundation. People who can sustain happiness and success have solid foundations and know the importance of strengthening and extending them when they are about to evolve and grow. Relationships provide numerous opportunities for evolution and growth - in fact, they actually propel this!

## NEEDS

Needs are what we '*must have*' to be our personal best. They are the driving force of our choices and behaviors, and the most important component in our personal foundation. To have needs is to be human. Individuals, consciously and unconsciously, seek every avenue to have their needs met. Getting them met is each individual's responsibility, not another's. For many, this is a missing skill.

Needs carry energy of urgency and a small amount of adrenalin. Although we don't consciously think about it, having them met is psychologically linked to our survival. Not having them met can make one feel anxious. This is not negative, but necessary. It's important to pay attention to our anxieties and learn to identity when we have an unmet need. Cutting off this natural warning sign creates stress, confusion and even despair in our lives.

Our core psychological and emotional needs are the most neglected and often invisible to us and to others. There are two reasons for this. Many feel embarrassed (shame) when they become aware of emotional needs and bury them with distracting or addictive behavior. Why are they embarrassed? Because their needs were either neglected in childhood or because a preoccupied or overwhelmed adult criticized their needs when they surfaced. In both cases the needs were unmet.

The other reason for their invisibility is that these core needs are so much a part of the essence of who we are, it doesn't occur to us to name them. We assume these are the same needs of all human beings, so we don't think we need to discuss them.

When an adult has unmet and unconscious needs from childhood, they will try to get these needs met either by another person or from a relationship. For example one might have unmet childhood needs for security, approval and to be cherished. This is the biggest mistake people make in relationships and causes more chaos and hurt than one could possibly imagine. Why? If you place one of your foundational (need) bricks in your relationship, the relationship will throw it out (because it doesn't belong there) and it usually hits you smack, bang in the head!

Unmet adult needs feel highly personal because they are often confused with unmet childhood needs. When *we* finally learn to meet our childhood needs, it takes away emotional hunger, which is often confused with love. I discuss this in more depth in Chapter 4, Breaking the Fantasy Bond.

If we don't learn to recognize our needs and get them met, we can become fearful, angry and even lose our confidence. When our needs aren't met, whether we know it or not, we feel like we won't survive and, more importantly, we don't thrive. If we don't thrive as individuals, then how can we possibly expect our relationships to thrive?

At the end of this chapter there are two exercises about needs that will help you clear up confusion in your relationships and begin building a strong personal foundation that fosters intimacy.

## VALUES

Values are what an individual considers innately worthwhile - *what we hold dear.* Awareness of our values helps us understand why particular things have great importance for us. When our values are fulfilled we feel like we are being true to ourself, our energy is increased and we are deeply satisfied.

Values are an internally generated code of ethics, meaning, you carry around inside of you your own version of society or your own model of the world. As long as you never violate that, you won't experience conflict. You can be counted on consistently. This is referred to as having a sense of honor.

Some of our core values are linked to and formulated by our childhood roles. In other words, there is a portion of the adapted childhood role that is very valuable to us. For example, a 'Hero' may value achievement or being responsible; a 'Caretaker' values being caring, loving and kind; a 'Surrogate Spouse' values relating and being in relationships; a 'Mascot' values playfulness, spontaneity and relieving tension; a 'Lost Child' values independence, autonomy and creativity; and a 'Scapegoat' values telling the truth and keeping relationships together at all costs.

On a deep, unconscious level we attach our value, our identity and even our sense of survival to our childhood roles. The danger here is that we can confuse the value in the childhood role for a need. The need energy placed behind the value generates reactive behavior, which blocks intimacy and creates conflict. In the next chapter there is an exercise called 'Intimacy, Values and Family Roles', which will shed more light on this issue.

(For more information on family roles and how they impact your life, see my first book *Set Yourself Free - a must read for people caught in addictive behaviors and those who love them. You can find this at* **http://www.SetYourselfFree.com.au**

Our values can evolve and change over time, particularly at different stages of our lives. However, our strongest values will only change if we intentionally choose to change them, usually because of a significant experience.

## WANTS

Wants are personal and can change with circumstances. A want is more like an objective with a strong intention. They are not as fixed or as exact as goals and usually don't have precise pictures. Wants are generated more from our values, which influence our choices. When we get them met, we feel alive and energized.

You will get what you want when you stay focused on your purpose and intention and don't let fear or other distractions take you off track. Before I met my husband, I spent some time reflecting on what my purpose and intention was to have a partner. I wanted companionship, a playmate and great sex. I also valued longevity and intimacy in relationships.

When I first met my husband he did not fit the image of the man I imagined I would have chosen for a partner. Pictures are usually constructed from our past. They can limit us. If I had stayed limited by my first impressions, I would not be in a great marriage today.

When we get what we want, it often involves an element of surprise. This is because we can't exactly determine what it precisely looks or feels like until it shows up.

## DESIRES

Desires motivate us and are what most people call goals. They are more precise and specific than wants and usually take longer to manifest. Within each desire is a need and a want. That's why desires are so desirable!

The need part of the desire is the driving force. It is the starting point. If you start to feel fear or anxiety, you are probably giving too much loyalty to the need part of your desire. This will limit you.

The want part of your desire is the purpose and intention. Ask yourself, 'What is my purpose and intention for this goal?' Then let your answer be the focal point of an action plan for meeting this goal. Staying focused will move you away from your fears and move you towards things that give you joy. Desires formed from value-based wants are the most fulfilling type of goals to achieve.

In Chapter 5, Creating Intimacy, there is a great exercise incorporating wants and desires in relationships.

People in happy, successful relationships possess an important secret: they are clear about the inner workings of what drives them (needs and desires), and they make value-based choices and decisions about what they want.

Here's an example of emotional and psychological needs, values, wants and desires as they pertain to relationships and relating with others:

## NEEDS, VALUES, WANTS, DESIRES: DIAGRAM 4

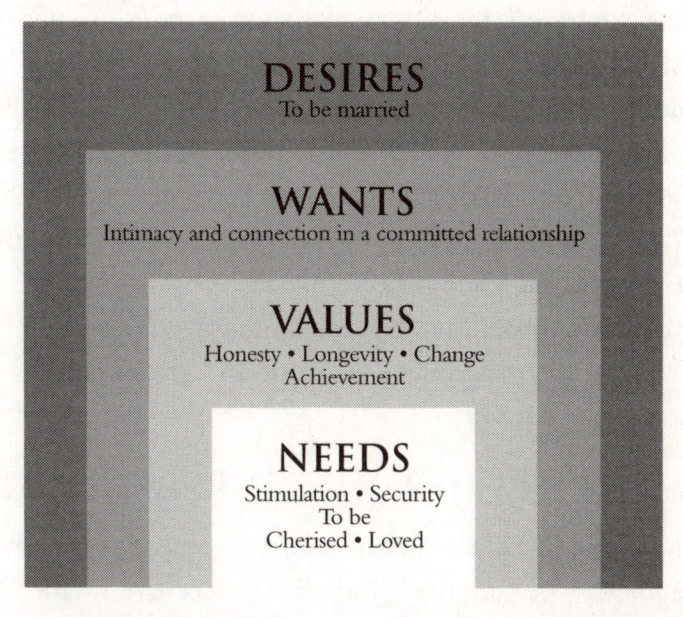

**DESIRES**
To be married

**WANTS**
Intimacy and connection in a committed relationship

**VALUES**
Honesty • Longevity • Change
Achievement

**NEEDS**
Stimulation • Security
To be
Cherished • Loved

Your needs are *stimulation, security,* to be *cherished* and *loved*. You discover that being cherished is an unmet childhood need. Once you release the pain from that, you find ways to *cherish* yourself. You determine what it takes to be *emotionally secure* and are open to learning *(stimulation)* to appreciate differences in others *(love)*.

You value *honesty, longevity* and *change*, realizing this is the important part from your childhood role of 'Scapegoat" that you want to keep. You also value *achievement*, which is not part of your childhood role.

You want to experience *intimacy* and *connection* in a *committed relationship*. This is not precise like a goal (desire), because intimacy, connection and a committed relationship could be characteristics in many different types of relationships, from colleagues to friends or a member of your family of origin.

You desire to be married. You are discerning about the type of partner and relationship that will fulfill your wants, considering the purpose and intention of the relationship (example of purpose and intention: you want to be married to have children, for religious reasons or to have 'safe sex'). Maybe your partner is someone who isn't rattled by change and likes to learn. You determine if there are some shared values and take time to evaluate this once the 'attraction phase' of the relationship moves to the 'power-struggle' stage. Perhaps you want a partner who is committed to resolving conflict and creating trust? This leads to intimacy and longevity, which you feel is a great achievement.

If you honestly don't know what your needs are, it can be helpful to go backwards from desires to wants and values and then look for the need inside them.

## IDENTIFYING DEPENDENT RELATIONSHIPS

Dependent people create dependent relationships - usually those with addictive personalities and those who love them. On the surface, one partner appears strong, together and in control. The other appears weaker, emotionally imbalanced and somewhat out of control. Unfortunately, society judges the second example to be the one with the problem.

The dictionary defines a dependent person as: 'relying on or requiring the aid of another for support'. Dependency in relationships can be healthy or unhealthy. Healthy dependency is known as inter-dependency (Diagram 2). Unhealthy dependency usually polarizes, one side being overly dependent and the other being counter-dependent (Diagram 3).

An overly dependent person relies on others to meet their needs and take care of them because they feel incapable of fully taking care of themselves. These people can't tell the difference between their needs, wants and desires and haven't got a clue about how to identify or meet their adult dependency needs.

On the surface, they appear selfless, insecure and lose themselves in relationships. Overly dependents pedestalize their partners because they feel inadequate and they are caretakers because of their desperate need to be needed. Having no boundaries, they allow others to invade their space.

The counter-dependent is the exact opposite of the above behavior. On the surface, a counter-dependent is a person who appears secure and independent, but inside they are fearful. This type of person requires support from others, praise and admiration, yet cannot tolerate others depending on them. Counter-dependents avoid and withdraw, causing confusion and becoming even more of a focal point for the overly dependent person. Having difficulty acknowledging any weaknesses within themselves, counter-dependents over-identify with strength and power.

Counter-dependents often feel superior to others and can be intrusive, invading others' boundaries without permission because they feel entitled to do so. They are self-centered, meaning that just about everyone and everything revolves around them or their life.

## CHARACTERISTICS OF POLARIZED, UNHEALTHY DEPENDENCY

| **Counter-dependent** | **Overly dependent** |
|---|---|
| 1. Self-centered | 1. Other-centered |
| 2. Intrusive | 2. Overly receptive |
| 3. Avoids/Withdraws | 3. Fuses/Enmeshes |
| 4. Escapes | 4. Entraps |
| 5. Persecutor | 5. Rescuer |
| 6. Alibi | 6. Enabler/covers up |
| 7. Child | 7. Caretaker |
| 8. Grandiosity | 8. Victims |
| 9. Dishonest about self | 9. Dishonest intentions |
| 10. Actively aggressive | 10. Passive aggressive |
| 11. Self will run riot | 11. Covertly manipulative |
| 12. Addicted to crisis | 12. Addicted to suffering |

Behind closed doors, sometimes these roles reverse - or sometimes the roles reverse later in a couple's life. Whether they do or not, both expressions of unhealthy dependency create instability and insecurity. Each partner *needs* the other to give a false sense of equilibrium.

Being *inter-dependent* in a relationship means we're able to give and receive support without compromising our own well-being and self-protection. When we have mastered self-protection, we can allow a trustworthy person to touch our souls or we can keep an untrustworthy person at arm's length.

## EXAMPLES OF UNHEALTHY, DEPENDENT ATTITUDES AND BEHAVIOR

1. **Feeling unable to leave the nest, or leaving it with uncomfortable feelings.**
   Many adults have this problem. Although they may have left home physically years ago, they have not left home emotionally and mentally. A healthy, inter-dependent person is able to move away from their family of origin without feeling guilty or to move closer to them without feeling absorbed or enmeshed.

2. **Feeling obligated to visit, telephone, entertain or chauffeur others around.**
   These activities can be enjoyable if done of your own volition, but they are not enjoyable when there is a 'should' attached to them. For example, many people spend Christmas with their parents when they would rather be socializing with their close friends.

3. **Asking permission of a partner for anything, including spending money, authority to speak, use of the car, etc.**
   This doesn't mean you shouldn't have agreements with each other about finances and the like, providing these agreements are reached in an adult manner together.

4. **Invasions of privacy, such as looking through doors and the wallets and private records of children or others.**
   This behavior is a violation of another's boundaries and is usually done because the person snooping is feeling insecure and fearful.

5. **Sentences like, 'I could never tell him how I feel' or 'She wouldn't like it'.**
   Dependent people will often tell their secrets to strangers or people they don't know well, or gossip about their close relationships. Instead, they should be communicating this information to their partner or other loved ones.

6. **Feeling committed to a particular job and unable to try anything else.**
   'I've worked in the family business all my life and they expect that of me' or 'I've gone to school for over eight years to be a doctor and although I'm really miserable and don't want to do it any more, I can't afford to do anything else.' Dependent people are too afraid to open themselves up to other possibilities and take a risk to do something else. They are always looking for a guarantee.

7. **Having expectations of how a spouse, parent or child ought to be or act, or being embarrassed by their appearance or behavior.**
   Because dependent people feel their family members are a reflection of themselves, they place too many expectations on them and then use controlling and manipulative tactics to have these fulfilled. How many parents feel uncomfortable being seen with their teenage children, especially if those children have purple hair, tattoos or body piercing? Or how does the pinstriped executive feel about taking his frumpy wife to the office party?

8.  **Being hurt by what others say, think, feel or do?**
    'What do you mean, you don't want to come over and be with me? That really hurt my feeling.' It's one thing to be disappointed when things don't go the way you'd like, but it's something else to lay guilt trips on people in order to get your own way. What's really happening in a situation like this is that the dependent person doesn't know how to get their needs met and they're afraid that if someone else doesn't do it for them, they won't feel fulfilled.

9.  **Feeling happy and successful only if your partner is feeling that way.**
    Maybe your partner is sad, angry or having a bad day. If you are a healthy person, you can still enjoy the flowers and trees on your afternoon picnic, rather than allowing his or her experience to spoil your day.

10. **Allowing someone else to make decisions for you or frequently asking for advice before you make a decision.**
    As a young adult, I had this problem because I had been told what to do my whole life. This is why we often feel uncertain and afraid to make the 'right' decisions as adults. Many of my adult clients have said to me, 'I don't know why I feel stupid. My parents never put me down.' No, perhaps they didn't do this verbally. But when a child is constantly told what to do and how to be, the unconscious message they pick up from this is, 'I don't know anything. I'm stupid'.

11. **Being obligated to others because you depend on them.**
    Some years ago, a business associate who was setting up seminars for me in another city, called to invite me to dine with him when he visited my city. Although my schedule was chock-a-block, I felt obligated to make time to see him because I was depending on the income he was generating for me. I cancelled and rescheduled a number of appointments

in order to attend the dinner. But it transpired that we had no opportunity to discuss business during the meal because he had invited others to join us and the evening turned into a party. I sat through it feeling resentful, but learned a valuable lesson.

12. **Not doing or saying something in front of a parent or dominant person for fear of their disapproval.**
For example, not smoking, drinking, swearing, eating sweets or being frank because you have a submissive role in that relationship.

13. **Using careful language, lying about your behavior or distorting the truth around a dominant person so they won't be upset with you.**
Walking on eggshells around people who matter to you is a complete energy drain. To be on guard to this degree is to try to control everyone and everything in your environment. There is a huge amount of stress involved in constantly *presenting* yourself in the way you think will win others' approval.

## PINPOINTING YOUR 'PAYOFFS'

If you've read the above checklist and identified with some of the behaviors and attitudes, you may wonder why, since they cause so much stress, you can't simply give them up. The answer is that these produce unhealthy 'rewards which have become an essential part of our modus operandi. These rewards are also known as 'hidden agendas' or 'payoffs'. To pinpoint your particular payoff, when you notice yourself in one of the above dependency patterns, stop and ask yourself what it is doing for you personally.

The following are some common payoffs born out of dependency patterns:

1. **Being dependent can keep you in the 'safe', protective custody of others and give you the 'little child' benefits of not being responsible for your own behavior.** If you're dependent on someone in this way, then when you make mistakes, you can claim it's not your fault. That way you don't have to face criticism or being put down. You give another all the power and then when anything goes wrong, the other person has to take care of it.

   This dependent behavior taught me an expensive lesson after my former husband and I started attending marriage counseling. Prior to this, I had been shouldering the majority of family responsibilities, including the managing of our income and the payment of our bills. I felt burned out from the pressure of so much responsibility and told my husband it was time for him to manage our finances. I then took on the childish role in our relationship, ran up our credit cards and depended on him to arrest the situation. He didn't, of course, and we incurred a great debt. My unconscious payoff in this situation was to feel relieved of over-responsibility and to be able to blame him for this mess. After all, I constantly reminded him, we'd never gotten into debt when *I'd* handled the finances.

2. **By staying dependent, you can blame your shortcomings on others.**

   Another way to say this is that we can keep our character defects. Character defects really are self-defense mechanisms. We've used some of our undesirable, negative behavior to protect ourselves because we have not learned a functional way to protect ourselves. If I stay dependent on you, I can abdicate my personal power and remain jealous, judgmental, afraid, defensive, indecisive and critical.

3. **If you are dependent on others, you don't have to undertake the hard work and risk of change. You are secure in your**

reliance on other people who will take responsibility for you. The payoff here is that while others control you, you don't have to experience the discomfort of learning the balance between letting go and being responsible.

4. **While you are pleasing others, you get to feel good about yourself.**
   As children, we learned that the way to be good was to please mummy and daddy and now many symbolic mummies and daddies manipulate us. This is the one which 'runs' the caretakers and people pleasers of the world. Their direct value is derived from what others think about them and from what they can do for others. Above all, they need to be needed and this people-pleasing behavior gives them that payoff.

5. **To avoid the guilt you sometimes feel when you act assertively, it is easier to 'behave' than to learn how to eliminate unhealthy guilt.**
   If you feel guilty when you assert yourself it is because you don't know that you have rights. The payoff is you don't have to face the shame you feel about not having certain rights.

6. **By modeling yourself on the parent, spouse or individual on whom you depend, you needn't make choices for yourself.**
   The payoffs here are that as long as you think what they think, or feel what they feel, there's no need for the hard work of determining what you think and feel and you don' feel responsible for any mistakes you make.

7. **Dependents would rather be followers than leaders because they are usually looking for the easier, softer way out.**
   As a follower, you can do what you're told and avoid trouble. It's simpler than taking all those risks that go with being your own person and facing the fear of failure. How many people resent tall poppies because they've dared to get out there and take a few risks in order to succeed?

The common thread in the above payoffs is the avoidance of personal responsibility. Think of responsibility as ... responding to your own ability.

People avoid responsibility because, sadly, they don't really believe they have what it takes to be responsible. And the reason for this is that most of them have had a heavy dose of shame.

Dependency is distasteful because it reduces you to less than a whole, independently functioning person. It may indeed be the easier, softer option in life, but it is by far the poorer one. Dependents miss out on the rich rewards of creating their lives the way they really desire them to be. They miss out on letting their true light shine.

## THE PANDORA PARADOX

After reading all of the above you may be feeling somewhat depressed or perhaps your situation looks a bit dreary? Maybe you've lost hope and don't know how to find it?

Hope is a spiritual quality, the expectation of good in the future. Hope is the call of humanity. Human beings look and pray for hope every day. For example, we hope for a 'better way' in the afterlife; to make good investments; to win the lotto; a healthy diagnosis from our doctor; to find our soul mate; to raise healthy children; or we visit the local clairvoyant in search of hope for a better future.

**Are you looking for hope? Well, look no more!**

My friend and colleague Marci Segal told me of her concept, 'The Pandora Paradox'. It's based on the mythological story of Pandora's Box.

Whether you know the story or not, when most people are asked what they know about Pandora's Box, the response is, 'It's a can of worms - don't open it!'. And for those who may not know, a paradox is something that is contradictory, but in fact is true.

As the story goes:

> *Pandora was the first woman on earth. The gods created her, a stunning beauty, with the gifts of intuition, curiosity, a playful spirit and ... a bit of deception! She was sent down to earth to punish man because the gods were angry about the way man was carrying on. Before she was sent, a final gift was given: a beautiful box with a gold cord tightly holding the lid closed. Pandora was given strict orders not to open the box or even lift the lid.*
>
> *Once on earth, Pandora heard voices calling to her from inside the box. Call it curiosity or intuition, eventually it got the best of her and she untied the cord and lifted the lid.*
>
> *The gods had malignantly crammed into this box all the diseases, sorrows, vices, crimes and misfortunes that afflict humanity. The box was no sooner opened than all these dark ills flew out, in the guise of horrid little brown-winged creatures, closely resembling moths. These creatures started stinging Pandora and her husband most unmercifully. They then flew out through the open door and windows, and fastened upon the merrymakers, whose shouts of joy were soon changed into wails of pain and anguish.*
>
> *Pandora and her husband had never before experienced the faintest sensation of pain or anger, but as soon as these winged evil spirits had stung them, they began to weep, and quarrel for the first time in their lives!*
>
> *In the midst of their quarrel, they suddenly heard a sweet little voice plead for freedom. The sound proceeded from the unfortunate box, whose cover Pandora had dropped again, in the first moment of her surprise and pain. 'Open, open, and I will heal your wounds! Please let me out!' the voice pleaded.*

CHAPTER 1: YOU - ME - WE

> *Pandora opened the box a second time and discovered that the gods, with a sudden impulse of compassion, had concealed among the dark, evil spirits one kindly, light creature - HOPE - which was at the bottom of the box! Hope touched the wounded places on Pandora and her husband, relieving their suffering. Then Hope quickly flew out of the open window to lift the downcast spirits of the merrymakers and heal them.*
>
> *According to the ancients, evil entered into the world bringing untold misery. But Hope followed closely in its footsteps, to aid struggling humanity, and point to a happier future.*

Maybe it's our intuition, or something of a spiritual nature that attracts us to opposites. Perhaps our soul is yearning to evolve and calling us to go through the darkness to get to the light?

The next time you feel trapped in a dark place of pain or confusion about a relationship - look within yourself and find the benefits from the light of Hope.

The hope is in your hands!

## ACCOUNTABLE ACTION

I like the saying, 'If nothing changes ... nothing changes!'. Doing the following three exercises will help you begin the process of setting yourself free in relationships.

To download free copies of the following exercises go to *http://www.SetYourselfFree.com.au/relationships/exercises.htm*

### ♡ EXERCISE 1: OBSERVING RELATIONSHIP PATTERNS

The purpose of this exercise is to examine your relationships to see if there is a common pattern or theme being re-enacted. The intention is for you to identify your part, so you can know where to begin to set yourself free.

Select three significant relationships, particularly one where there has been a conflict that was not resolved. The relationships may be romantic, close friends, business clients, colleagues, or family members. Past relationships are preferable, but you may use current ones.

Take one person at a time and respond to the following questions:

1. Who was/is the dominant person in the relationship? (Who made the first move; took the lead most of the time; made most of the decisions?)

   _____

2. Who was the follower or the more compliant one?

   _____

3. What attracted you initially?

   _____

4. What was your purpose and intention for the relationship?

   _____

5. What was the theme of the relationship? (Was there a lot of intensity, was it boring, or highly sexual, was it centered on dependent behavior, were there issues about abandonment or engulfment?).

   _____

6. What metaphor or fairytale would best describe this relationship?

   _____

7. How did the relationship end, or what is the current state of the relationship?

   _____

Once you have answered the above seven questions for each relationship, discern and write the answers:

- What similarities do these relationships share?
- What differences do these relationships have?
- Were the differences created pro-actively or reactively?

## ♡ EXERCISE 2: ASSESSING YOUR UNMET NEEDS

The purpose of the following is for you to identify your unmet psychological and emotional needs regarding relationships. This is the first step to creating a strong personal foundation, which is essential to having intimate, healthy relationships.

When it comes to needs, it's important to identify and distinguish between your unmet childhood needs as well as unmet needs in your adult life. Normally, people have a fair amount of resistance to doing this. Because of this, you may find that you are easily distracted while doing the exercise. If so, persist. The third exercise will most likely unveil the resistance.

Find a quiet place where you will be undisturbed. When doing the exercise it's important to focus, be as specific as you can. Try not to complicate your thought processes. Often the first thing that comes to mind or what you feel embarrassed to admit, is a true need.

On the right is a list of emotional and psychological needs. This is just a small list to get you started. There are many more needs than what appear below. Review the list. Notice if you feel any energy or judgments (either positive or negative) about any of the particular needs. Circle the ones you feel are yours, whether they are met or unmet needs.

| | | |
|---|---|---|
| Being loved | Being cherished | Get attention |
| Security | Sense of belonging | Responsibility |
| Duty | Membership | Acting on impulses |
| Freedom | Self-expression | Self-esteem |
| Confidence | Order | Structure |
| Rules | Stimulation | Excitement |
| Mastery | Self-control | Knowledge |
| Competence | Understanding | Acceptance |
| Being acknowledged | Being right | Control |
| Luxury | Prosperity | Abundance |
| Meaning | Significance | Being unique |
| Clarity | Certainty | Unity |
| Co-operation | Harmony | Balance |
| Beauty | Authenticity | Privacy |
| Power | Respect | To win |
| Acknowledgement | Encouragement | Accuracy |
| Friendship | Success | Achievement |
| Self-actualization | Connection | Commitment |
| Spirituality | Inspiration | Learning |
| Being appreciated | Making an impact | Compassion |
| Tenderness | Fierceness | Playfulness |
| Spontaneity | Trust | Stability |
| Being heard | Being liked | Being valued |

**Close your eyes and take some deep breaths. Drop into your body and find your center. Once you do this, open your eyes and answer the questions below.**

1. **Childhood**
    Reflect back on your childhood (i.e. birth to 18 years). What needs are you aware of that were not met in your childhood?

CHAPTER 1: YOU – ME – WE

2. **Adulthood**
   What adult needs are you aware of that are not being met now?

   _____

## ♡ EXERCISE 3: FACING AND EMBRACING YOUR NEEDINESS AND NEEDLESSNESS

The first step in being accountable is to get your needs met. The purpose of this exercise is for you to gain clarity and to be honest about your needy and/or needless behavior, and the impact it has in your relationships. The intention is for you to make decisions about how you will change your behavior.

### PART 1: BE CLEAR

1. In what relationships have you been feeling and/or acting out your neediness or needlessness?

   _____

2. Specifically how do you act?

   _____

3. When you react in a needy or needless way, what payoffs are you receiving? What does this behavior do for you?

   _____

4. What are the consequences of this behavior?

   _____

5. Do you use needy or needless behavior to manipulate others? If so, how?

   _____

### PART 2: BE HONEST

Negative behavior patterns (especially regarding our needs) usually come from childhood patterns. The grooves of these patterns are deep and their melodies play out in our adult lives. As adults, we have denial/ignorance about our patterns and can be quite upset when we discover we have been 'playing the same song' for most of our lives.

Remember, children are needy by nature, not by choice. Go within and ask your needy inner child, or the most vulnerable part of you, to take you back into the past so that you may clearly identify any emotional upsets that are linked to your needy/needless behavior. Allow yourself to view it from your adult perspective with compassion and curiosity.

Have the adult you ask the following questions of your vulnerable, inner child, letting the child respond. It is helpful to write your answers with your non-dominant hand.

6. What do you need or want?

   _____

7. What are you upset/angry/hurt/frightened about?

   _____

8. Who do you think should pay for this?

   _____

9. What do you do to get your way?

   _____

10. How are you getting attention and acting out in your life?

    _____

11. Tell the child in your own words, I am here to help you, but you have to let go and let me take charge. Then ask the child, 'Are you willing to trust me?' 'Why?' 'Why not?' (Listen to what your child has to say and write it down).

    _____

12. Respond to your child in a loving manner. Do something comforting and then say goodbye.

---

## PART 3: DISCERN

Take your adult self to a place in nature where you can do some soul searching. You can do this literally or in your imagination.

13. What effect has your wounded, needy child had on your life as an adult? (Consider beliefs, feelings, behaviors.)

14. Regarding your neediness/needlessness, how are you the same today as you were as a child? How are you different?

15. List the benefits you would gain if your needy/needless inner child were not in charge and unconsciously driving you.

16. What resources are available to you today that you didn't have as a child? List as many as you can think of.

17. What steps of change will you take so that you don't have to continue to react in this needy/needless way? What will you do differently?

**After completing the above three exercises it is healing and confirming to share what you just experienced and the insights you gained with someone you trust.**

# CHAPTER 2

# ANCHORS AWAY

*Perhaps the greatest lesson is to lessen
the need to have the present look like the past.*

The Story Teller

'I don't know why, but I just feel like I have to get away,' said Mark. 'I love Lisa, she's a really beautiful person. God, my family even loves her. It just doesn't feel right to marry her.'

'I can't believe I've done it again,' said Karen. 'Dan seemed so different than my past partners. We didn't even have sex for the first few months we dated. My Mom was right, you just can't trust men!'

'I'm sick of this! It's happened again! I can't believe it!' Client after client sit in front of me baffled by familiar, recurring relationship problems. It's as if they were anchored to past patterns - like a ship at the dock unable to sail to its destination. Being anchored to the past stops you from truly being present and creating the relationships you desire.

An anchor is something that holds something in place or links things together. Anchors seem positive when offering security or negative if they are holding you back. If a ship is not ready to set sail or needs to stay stationary in a great fishing spot, then an anchor can be seen as positive. However, if you're at the dock, ready to set sail and despite all your effort, you can't pull up anchor, then it can be seen as a negative.

Today most of us realize that our past clearly influences our present. Adapted childhood roles; negative and limited beliefs; unresolved feelings and un-useful behaviors keep people anchored to the past, recycling the same relationship patterns. If you're not happy and satisfied in your relationships, then it is important to examine these and uncover what is causing you disappointment, frustration and misery.

> *'If you cannot get rid of the family skeleton,
> you might as well make it dance.'*
> George Bernard Shaw

## FAMILIAR OR FAMILY?

Most of what we learned about relationships and relating happened in our family of origin, in our formative years. Just like an adult's personal foundation, the family has a foundation as well. The most important thing to understand about your family's foundation is this:

It is the **relationship** of the parents that provides the foundation for the family.

Parents with faulty relationships (for whatever reason) provide damaged foundations for their family. Sure, you may realize you have unresolved issues with your mother or father, however, the adapted roles you took on in childhood to fill the cracks in your family's faulty foundation, cause far more chaos in your adult relationships than you can imagine. Why? Because this dynamic happens on the unconscious level and most people have had little or no education about this.

This is why a good number of adults have weak personal foundations. You only have to think about how your parents related to each other when you were growing up and any other dynamics in their relationship, to start to understand why there are missing bricks in your personal foundation.

It's true - most parents did the best they could for their children and the whole family. The majority of them were too emotionally damaged in their formative years to provide a healthy climate for their children. In the many years I've worked with family dynamics, I've realized that no one is to blame. This even includes parents who deserted their children or parents who were very nasty and mean. When you explore their childhoods more closely, you'll find that they were very wounded.

Families with cracks in their foundation cling together in order to survive. They become enmeshed. An individual's personal needs and values are sacrificed to keep the family together. In an enmeshed family system each member unconsciously plays out different roles, thereby giving up his or her own, unique authentic self because they are adapting their personality and don't get the chance to discover their true emotional needs. The roles fill in the cracks and the child's personal needs are unmet. This is why it is such a difficult task for countless adults to identify and meet their needs.

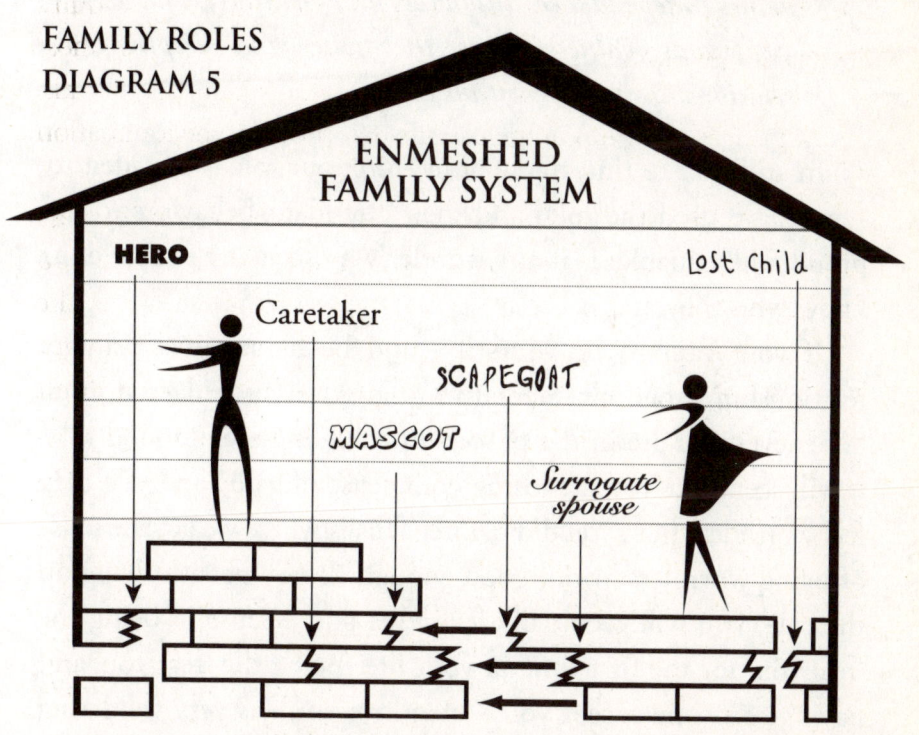

**FAMILY ROLES**
**DIAGRAM 5**

### ENMESHED FAMILY SYSTEM

HERO · Caretaker · SCAPEGOAT · MASCOT · Surrogate spouse · Lost child

The parent's **relationship** is the family's foundation.

## CHAPTER 2: ANCHORS AWAY

Eliminating the 'roles' you took on in your formative years is one of the most important things you can do to free yourself from relationship dynamics that anchor you to the past. This is easier said than done because within each role is a value - usually a core value of the one who took on the adapted role. It's hard to separate ourselves from our values, as I discussed in chapter 1.

*Some of our core values are linked to and formulated by our childhood roles. In other words, there is a portion of the adapted childhood role that is very valuable to us. For example, a 'Hero' may value achievement or being responsible; a 'Caretaker' values being caring, loving and kind; a 'Surrogate Spouse' values relating and being in relationships; a 'Mascot' values playfulness, spontaneity and relieving tension; a 'Lost Child' values independence, autonomy and creativity; and a 'Scapegoat' values telling the truth and keeping relationships together at all costs.*

In addition to this, many of us think our role is our identity - and have used the roles and their attendant behaviors to feel proud and valuable. Is it any wonder why so many people don't know who they are?

If you want to be yourself - and be happy in a primary relationship - then it's imperative to give up your adapted roles. Whenever you are in the process of shedding a childhood role, it will seem like you are losing your sense of value and you may feel worth less than you did before. This is where we get the sense of being worthless or not good enough. If you persist giving up the role, you will eventually feel relief and a sense of being the 'real you' for the first time in your life. Being the 'real you' and having someone accept you - even love you - is very validating and makes you feel wonderful.

When my husband and I were first dating, he went along with me to a radio talkback program I was the guest on. After we left, I said to him that one of the things I'd always wanted to do was take voice lessons, so I could be more professional and effective with my voice. I was surprised when he immediately responded, 'I wouldn't do that if I were you.'

'Why?' I asked.

'I had my eyes closed when I was listening to you, and when you were speaking to the callers, there was a real quality of compassion in your voice,' he said. 'I'd be afraid that the voice lessons would mask the real you from coming through.'

When he said that, I felt a tingle inside and was surprised that he noticed. After years of marriage, when I look back to our courting days, this is one of my fondest memories.

The late Virginia Satir also identified patterns of behavior, ones used under stress, which are known as 'The Satir Categories'. One of her students, Sharon Wegscheider-Cruse, developed the family roles in her early work with children of alcoholic families, which has since been expanded upon over time by other professionals. Below are some examples of the roles we adopt in childhood. There may be several others not listed.

| HERO | MASCOT |
| --- | --- |
| Little adult | Class clown |
| Super responsible | Distracter |
| Over-achiever | Rascal |
| The star | Busy bee |
| The saint | Cute one |
| Super athlete | Entertainer |
| Genius | Comedian |
| Leader | |

CHAPTER 2: ANCHORS AWAY

| SCAPEGOAT | SURROGATE SPOUSE |
|---|---|
| Troublemaker | Confidant |
| Rebel | Listener |
| Angry child | Enabler |
| Focal point | Little princess |
| Acting-out child | Advisor |
| Under-achiever | Dad's partner |
| Victim | Mature one |
| Addict | Mom's little man |
| Misfit | Daddy's little girl |

| LOST CHILD | CARETAKER |
|---|---|
| Invisible | Peacemaker |
| Daydreamer | Little parent |
| Good girl/boy | Family referee |
| Invisible | Dutiful |
| Perfect one | Mediator |
| Isolator | Makes sacrifices |
| Loner | Placator |
| Sick one (Physical) | Worrier |
| Adjusting child | Giving one |

## BELIEFS

'It's done unto you as you believe.' I've found this ancient truth to be amazingly true! Another wise saying I learned from one of my first teachers, Terry Cole Whittaker, is *'The physical universe never lies.'* She used to say, 'If you don't know what your thoughts and beliefs are, just look at your life. *Your life is an outer expression of what you deeply believe.'*

I say, just look at your relationships and how you interact. That will really show you what you believe about yourself, others (men, women and especially people who are different from you) and relationships. How have your beliefs shown up?

## LIMITING BELIEFS

The problem with limiting and negative beliefs is that we bury them because they cause us to feel hopeless, helpless or worthless. We usually bury them so well that we may not realize we even have a certain negative belief.

According to Robert Dilts, recognized internationally as one of the foremost developers, trainers and practitioners of Neuro-Linguistic Programming, the most common limiting belief issues tend to fall into one of the following three groups:

1. **Hopelessness:** This is a belief that the desired goal is not achievable regardless of your capabilities.

2. **Helplessness:** This is a belief that the desired goal is possible but that you are not capable of achieving it.

3. **Worthlessness:** This is a belief that you do not deserve the desired goal because of something you are or have not done.

Negative thinking and critical judgments are generated from limiting beliefs. Left to run riot, negative thinking can turn into mental obsession. When we mentally obsess, it takes us out of our bodies and feelings and puts us into our heads. People who mentally stew on something don't realize they do this to medicate overwhelming feelings and catastrophic thoughts.

Your most limiting beliefs *will* show up in your relationships, especially your intimate relationships or those you spend a great deal of time with (like at work). These limiting beliefs drive your reactive behaviors, which greatly affect your ability to relate in healthy ways. Reactive behaviors can also take the form of non-action, or being frozen.

Here are some examples of limiting beliefs showing up in relationship beliefs:

Bob and Mary communicate effectively with their colleagues and both run financially successful business departments. However, when they disagree about finances at home, they often have nasty fights (hopeless).

'All my friends tell me that I am such a fantastic person and a good catch, how come I am still single?' (hopeless)

'A lot of people have good relationships, but I'll bet they didn't come from a family like mine!' (helpless)

'I'm 35 years old, still renting and living from week to week. Why would a woman want to marry me?' (worthless).

## FEELINGS

Unresolved feelings from past relationships, whether from our childhood or as adults, cause us to overreact or to re-enact past patterns of behavior. Identifying our feelings can be quite confusing and expressing our feelings in an appropriate manner is even more perplexing. Our feeling reality is by far the most impaired part of us and for that reason, I have written more about them in this section than I have on Beliefs, Family and Behaviors.

If you want to be calm, confident and happy in your primary relationships, it's important to learn about feelings and how to express them appropriately as adults. Buried, carried, frozen or overwhelmed feelings will always cause problems in relationships, not to mention make you physically ill. I also believe this is the main reason such a high percentage of people are taking anti-depressants.

The following is an excerpt from my first book, *Set Yourself Free,* which I have tailored for this book with relationships in mind. I've selected this piece because it speaks directly to the fundamental problem with feelings in our primary relationships. This is a summary from Pia Mellody's groundbreaking work on feelings and how they apply to co-dependent and love-addicted relationships.

## ADULT FEELINGS

Our basic raw feelings are joy, fear, pain, loneliness and anger. Guilt, lust and shame are a combination of thinking and feeling realities, but they are so pervasive in our lives that for our purposes I've included them as basic raw feelings.

Healthy, mature adults are able to identify and express their raw feelings in a mature, responsible way without overreacting to people or situations, even when others try to 'push their buttons'.

Being able to exercise positive self-control with our feelings will provide us with the energy, intuition, protection, growth and freedom that most of us are looking for. Relationships are our emotional food and knowing how to bring our feelings into everyday relating gives us a stronger connection.

## CARRIED FEELINGS

All of our feelings are positive and give us special gifts. In childhood we learned to unconsciously take on and 'carry' the feelings of other people. Because of this, we may distort, become overwhelmed by or overreact when we express our feelings. This confusion has caused us to judge many of our feelings as negative.

We experience these overwhelmed, carried feelings as:

**Hysterical elation:** rather than **Joy**

**Panic or paranoia:** rather than **Fear**

**Hopelessness or suffering:** rather than **Pain**

**Isolation:** rather than **Loneliness**

**Rage:** rather than **Anger**

**Immobility or desperate apologies:** rather than **Guilt**

**Greedy, obsessive desire:** rather than **Lust**

**Worthlessness:** rather than **Shame**

Understanding and releasing carried feelings is vital to developing healthy, balanced relationships. How did we carry feelings in the first place?

When a major caregiver is irresponsible *with or in denial of* his or her feelings, the feelings being denied or handled irresponsibly will be unconsciously picked up and carried by the children in the vicinity. This happens especially when a child is being abused or neglected in anyway. This is why children who've been abused usually feel intensely dirty, ashamed and afraid. They are carrying the shame that their perpetrator couldn't feel when they were abusing them.

Most of the overwhelmed feelings that surface once we stop suppressing them aren't even ours! Through progressively releasing the carried feelings, expressing and embracing our adult feelings, we will begin to feel a greater sense of freedom in our lives, have more control over reactive behavior and therefore have healthier relationships.

## ADULT-TO-ADULT FEELING EXCHANGE

It is possible to break the childhood pattern of carrying feelings for others by establishing emotional boundaries. There is more information on boundaries and how to set them up in Chapter 5, Creating Intimacy.

Damaged emotional boundaries are an epidemic in our world today. The lack of boundaries causes people to pick up and carry other peoples' feelings in the present. We do this by unconsciously exchanging, carrying and often acting out the feelings of the adults to whom we are close. In particular, we do this in the same manner in which, during childhood, we carried feelings from our caregivers.

So, how do you identify if you are carrying another's feelings and what do you do about it if you discover that you are? Usually, these feelings don't seem to fit the experience. They can make you feel embarrassed, confused and overwhelmed. You will often notice that the person you are carrying the feelings for isn't very emotional about the related issue and you are overly emotional, when the issue isn't even yours. This 'I feel for you' experience goes way beyond compassion. The following example illustrates this point.

Years ago my boyfriend Chad was cleaning out his closet when he came upon an old photo album. Chad had been close to his mother, who had died many years before I met him. Chad was a lovely man, but not very emotionally expressive. Smiling as he gazed at a photo of his mother, he said, 'Oh, there's my sweet, beautiful Mom. God, how I miss her.' His face had a glazed-over expression on it as if he were looking at a beautiful princess (mind you, this man was in his late thirties). He passed the picture to me and I nearly fell over when I looked at it. His mother was the epitome of a chronic alcoholic - swelled belly, swollen face and nose, broken capillaries and all, plus skinny bird legs and a cigarette hanging out of her mouth!

Shocked, I managed a smile while handing the picture back. Chad continued gazing at the picture with a transfixed look on his face. Then, something strange happened. Tears started welling up in my eyes, which I couldn't stop. Embarrassed, I made a lame excuse and went into another room. It only took a few minutes to realize that I had carried Chad's pain about his mother. Not necessarily the pain of her death, but the buried pain from a little boy who desperately needed mothering from a mother who couldn't be present (the mother wound). I closed my eyes, centered myself and took some deep breaths, focusing my awareness on where I actually held his pain in my body. With intent, I took more deep breaths, took his pain and handed it back to him. I imagined him receiving his pain and being able to deal with it.

A while later, Chad seemed agitated and went to lie down

because he said he had a headache. *Feelings are muscle bound and if we don't express them, we often dump them into our bodies.* Later we talked about the situation and when Chad spoke about his mother, he actually cried. Embarrassed, he wiped his eyes saying, 'Gee, I don't know where that came from.' I did!

This syndrome is particularly identifiable in marriage/couple counseling. Many times when couples come in, the man is cool, collected and controlled and the woman is an angry, emotional basket case. He seems to think the problem is that his wife needs to pull herself together and has come to counseling primarily to support her to do that. Meanwhile, *she's* bought into the idea that she's the problem and begins to question her own sanity.

In probing beneath the superficial circumstances of this type of case, I often find that the man has refused to acknowledge and express his feelings and therefore the woman is carrying and acting out his unexpressed feelings. She will particularly do this for him in the same way that she did it for the parent he most resembles, for example, his mother was never angry, his father was never sad and neither ever expressed shame.

On the other hand, we've all known women who profess that they don't get angry. They present an unfailingly jolly and optimistic face to the world and if you ask them how they are, will mostly respond: 'Fine, just fine.' Often such women have partners who are raging maniacs. They have unconsciously chosen men like this, so that they can get indirect relief from their repressed anger (as the man acts it out) while outwardly they remain a 'saint'.

## UNRESOLVED CHILDHOOD FEELINGS

We bury our unresolved feelings from our childhood until life intervenes and uncovers them, forcing us to deal with them. When these old feelings surface, and they will in our closest relationships, we find they are alive and well! A good book I once read expressed this beautifully in its title, *'Feelings Buried Alive Never Die.'*

The degree to which our childhood feelings weren't expressed and validated is the degree to which they are locked inside of us and frozen. When we allow ourselves to recall and identify our frozen feelings from childhood, it feels as if we're thawing out. However, all of our frozen childhood feelings obviously will not thaw out overnight. Initially, it can be a slow process. But once the floodgates open, it's important to remember that this is a time to be gentle with yourself, as these feelings are vulnerable and need to be acknowledged and purged. I recommend that people get instruction and professional support to express and release frozen childhood feelings.

Sometimes, when we become aware of and begin to feel our frozen feelings, we childishly want to express them to our parents or siblings and demand that they acknowledge them. Doing this is usually disastrous because while it confronts the dysfunction in the family system, it also triggers more confusion, suppression and denial. Additionally, be aware that analyzing our past and debating with our families can be a defensive mental process which takes us out of our *feelings* and into our heads. And then we're right back where we started.

## BEHAVIORS

Something I learned from Neuro-Linguistic Programming has profoundly changed my life and the life of many of my clients. It's this:

*Change happens on the neurological level - not the logical level.*

In other words, we may not be able to change behaviors just because we 'know better' or logically determine that 'we should'. Nevertheless, we can make changes that we find emotionally or mentally challenging by using our physiology - our bodies.

Again, I recall wise words from my teacher, Terry Cole Whittaker. 'One day I was sitting on the couch for hours trying to figure out my problems when I suddenly realized that I had to get up off the couch first,' she said. Just doing something different can interrupt an un-useful behavior pattern and start you down a different path. You may not know where you're going when you start, but you'll soon discover that you are led, a step at a time, in the right direction.

Behaviors can be active or passive, meaning what we *do* or *don't do*. I like to think of negative behaviors as un-useful behaviors. These are behaviors that have outlived their 'use-by date'.

There are three types of *un-useful* behaviors:

**Distracting behaviors:** These take us off focus, either delaying or preventing us from achieving happiness, satisfaction and success. Distracting behaviors reduce mental sharpness, productivity and leave people feeling tired and lethargic. An example of a distracting behavior is spending too much time in front of the computer or TV, rather than having an intimate conversation with your partner or even making love.

**Destructive behaviors:** These cover all of the above, as well as hurt or cause harm to another or to oneself. Destructive behaviors can be conscious and deliberate or unconscious and reactive. Just because a person does not have a conscious intent to be destructive, doesn't remove their responsibility and accountability for it. An example of destructive behavior is stooping so low by dipping into your children's college fund to pay off debts; or raging at your partner when you don't get your way, rather than discussing the conflict with the willingness to work something out.

**Addictive behaviors:** These behaviors are a combination of distracting and destructive behaviors, which form a pattern that can be identified. Clearly identifying addictive behaviors requires education, careful analysis and involves giving up self-defence mechanisms. Addictive behaviors are progressive and get worse over time, although some fool themselves by switching from a plentiful repertoire. Addictions are processes of decreasing choice. At first, addictions give us the illusion of consistency, but eventually they make us feel like victims.

An example of this is Helen discovering her new husband is the fourth man to cheat on her. Helen probably doesn't realize that she is co-addicted to being in relationships with addictive people, in this case probably a sex addict or an avoidant personality.

## THE MISSING LINK

Addictions and people with addictive personalities are a huge reason that so many relationships crash or never even get off the ground. Chapter 3, The Romance Trance, discusses the different types of addictions that pertain to relationships. However, in all my years of working with people and their relationship challenges, I have found that denial and the lack of knowledge about addiction, co-addiction and the addictive personality is the *missing link* in getting clear on how to stop the misery and start relating in happy, healthy ways. For this reason, I want to go into this topic in more depth.

Untreated addictions and addictive personalities are the reason that most marriage counseling doesn't work. Either the professional doesn't know how to identify the addictive pattern or the couple drops off from the counseling without resolving much because they are tired of swinging back and forth like a pendulum. For years, literally hundreds of clients have confided in me that they couldn't find anyone to help them understand the addictive process they were caught in.

## CHAPTER 2: ANCHORS AWAY

Most professional counselors, psychologists, doctors and other health practitioners do not know how to treat addicts or their partners, unless they specialize in addiction treatment. The problem is that professionals who do, usually only specialize in treating specific addictive disorders such as alcoholism/chemical dependency, compulsive gambling, sex addiction, bulimia or anorexia and so on. They are not trained to help the addictive personality in general. This is important because addicts are good at covering and switching addictions just when they are about to be caught, or an addiction has caused such harmful consequences that they had to switch to something else.

There is a difference between abusing something and being addicted to it. Abuse takes the easy way out and looks for the softer way. This provides a crutch to relieve pressure and put aside fears. *There is an element of laziness when we are abusing something.* In order to give up the crutch we must actively take steps to embrace our fears and deal with resentments. *With addiction, there is frustration rather than laziness.* Addicts are addicted to their substance or process, because they don't see that there is another way to function.

There is also a difference between compulsive and addictive personalities, and being an addict. When we are being compulsive there is the strong illusion of being *in* control. When we are addicted we have lost control.

John Bradshaw says, 'Compulsive, addictive behaviors are not about being hungry, thirsty, horny or needing work. *They are about mood alteration.* Compulsive, addictive behaviors help us manage our feelings. They distract us or alter the way we are feeling so we don't have to feel the loneliness and emptiness of our abandonment and shame.'

Vernon Johnson, author of the book *I'll Quit Tomorrow* (which is considered to be the best available model for the treatment of the disease of alcoholism,) has defined alcoholism and chemical dependency *as an addiction to mood-altering chemicals. The most significant characteristics of the disease are: it is primary, predictable, progressive, chronic and fatal.*

David Smith, from the Haight Ashbury Free Clinic in San Francisco California, defines an addict as *'anyone who continues to use any substance or process in spite of adverse consequences.'*

There are two categories of addictions: substance addictions and process addictions. *Substance addictions* such as alcoholism/chemical dependency (nicotine, caffeine, narcotics, whether they are prescription or recreational drugs) or eating disorders, *involve ingesting or injecting a substance into the body.*

*Process addictions* include work addiction, compulsive gambling, spending and shopping, love-addicted relationships, religious addiction and sex addiction, or you can be addicted to thinking, raging, rushing/adrenalin, creating crises/dramas or being busy. Sometimes a process and substance are components of the same addictions. For example, there are many rituals associated with eating and serving food.

*With process addictions people are engaged in ritualistic behaviors where the mood alteration comes from the process of performing a series of actions.* For example, the high that a compulsive gambler gets when his or her horse wins is only part of the payoff. The rest comes through the ritualistic 'process' of reading the form guide, phoning contacts for tips, selecting a bookmaker and placing the bet. Similarly, for the sex addict, the seduction process, cruising, obsessing and fantasizing, become as big a payoff as orgasm.

Much research and many statistics have been collected and many books written about addictions. Education is the first step in coming out of denial. Through education, people have been able to drop their moral judgments regarding addictions and develop a more mature understanding of their cause and treatment. If you suspect that you have an addictive personality or an addiction, then I suggest you seek treatment. My first book, *Set Yourself Free*, provides education and treatment for the addictive and co-addictive person. For a time, addictions and compulsive behavior may give you the illusion of consistency, survival or even winning, but in the end you and those with whom you are involved will always lose!

The key to setting yourself free from the anchors that hold you back from having healthy relationships is to know how to grieve. Once you have processed your unresolved grief from past losses, you will be able to consciously choose and change your beliefs to match and support your values. You will be able to understand your feelings and know how to manage and express them appropriately. You will more easily identify and replace unuseful behaviors that no longer serve you. That's why I call the process - *Good Grief!*

## GOOD GRIEF!

*'Good grief' is what I call a dynamic healing process of transformation.* It involves examining, uncovering and changing beliefs; buried feelings and the destructive/addictive behaviors these generate.

Grief is a state of expression regarding loss. Loss of our authentic self, vocation/career, missed opportunities, self-expression, relationships, health, money, sexuality, and ability to have children - the list goes on. Grief work is not just about expressing your feelings or sitting with the feelings. That's misery! It is about freeing yourself from unresolved issues from the past pertaining to loss.

Except when there is a death or loss of a primary relationship, most people do not know how to allow themselves to grieve or understand the importance of grieving. Instead, people usually bury their feelings and later combine them with negative beliefs about something to do with the loss. These turn into resentments and regrets.

When we don't know how to deal with loss or missed opportunities, we tend to hold on to resentments and regrets. This causes us to be seen as victims or branded as a 'negative person', usually a troublemaker. Another way we do not deal with our grief is to download our grievance stories to anyone who will listen, which makes us become more depressed or physically ill. Recycling and wallowing in resentments and grievance stories releases stress chemicals from the brain, causing us to feel beaten down and hopeless about a situation. This clouds our vision to possibilities of moving on and overcoming the upset or disappointment that fuelled the resentment/grievance in the first place.

Not knowing how to live with loss and process unresolved grief keeps one recycling misery blocked by negative/limited thinking and trapped in un-useful behaviors that cause more disappointment, misery and pain.

Unresolved grief drives us to:

- Distraction
- Destruction
- Addiction

Distracting, destructive and addictive behavior patterns are unconscious psychological defenses that take significant energy to keep in place, not to mention how they also sabotage our happiness and success.

Albeit the defense mechanisms work for a time, eventually these behaviors cease to do the job of defending the unresolved grief. This causes people to feel desperate, overwhelmed and out of control. The answer is to learn how to resolve the grief, which then lets you more easily make the changes you need to make and feel in control while making them.

The exercises at the end of each chapter have been carefully designed to help you set yourself free from unresolved grief. I suggest you find a buddy, coach, counselor or facilitator who can support you through this process. We have several coaches and facilitators whom I have trained who can support you. Go to *http://www.SetYourselfFree.com.au* for information on this service.

## SELF-CARE WHILE HEALING UNRESOLVED GRIEF

Although it is 'good' and healthy for you to grieve, most people don't know how to take good care of themselves during the grieving process. The following suggestions for good self-care during the grieving process will help you get through the experience with more ease and self-control.

1. **Pay attention to what your body is telling you.** If you need to sleep then do so. If you need to cry, cry. Freely express your emotions with people who will listen with compassion and have been in similar situations. Most importantly, honor all of your emotions and go with the flow.

2. **Lower expectations of yourself.** You can't expect to run at full capacity when you are in this healing process. Give yourself a break and don't expect to perform as well as you normally do for a while. Let others know that it may take a bit of time before your performance is back to normal.

3. **Communicate your needs.** Don't expect others to know what you need. Communicate to your family and friends and let them know how they can support you. Give feedback to people so that they will continue to do what is working.

4. **Take time to do the things you need to do for yourself.** Engage in activities that are healing and nurturing to your soul. Spend extra time caring for your needs.

5. **Pamper yourself.** Treat yourself extra well at this time. Without breaking your budget, do things for yourself that are helpful. Being with people who are nurturing to you, taking hot baths, extra time in the shower, massage, meditation, long walks at the beach or any other inexpensive activity will help to nurture your soul and protect your finances while you are indulging in this down time.

6. **Keep a personal journal.** Writing down your thoughts and feelings can help you to validate your losses. Journaling is a powerful way to pour out your grief, often bringing clarity and resolution.

7. **Eat properly and get plenty of sleep.** Maintaining a healthy diet and getting proper sleep is essential for functioning as well as you can. If you are having difficulty, get a check-up from your doctor, naturopath or holistic practitioner.

8. **Get physical exercise.** If you exercised prior to this time, try to maintain the same routine. If you weren't exercising, start! Moving your body helps to move the feelings out. It will also help you to sleep and maintain physical balance, which is essential to feeling grounded. If you are overweight or have health problems, visit your doctor before embarking on a physical exercise routine.

9. **Be aware of others' reactions.** Many people do not know how to react appropriately to your grief. Some are more comfortable than others in responding to people who are in an emotive state. Be true to yourself and let others know if they say something inappropriate.

**If you need extra support, such as individual counseling or coaching, get it.** Get all the support you need. Once you have opened up to the grieving process, you can go through it quite quickly with a skilled counselor, coach or facilitator. Making this investment can save you a lot of heartache and get you back on your feet more quickly. It is normal for feelings of hopelessness or even suicidal thoughts to surface at this time. Don't hesitate to contact a professional and talk about these feelings and thoughts so they may pass and you don't feel crazy.

## ACCOUNTABLE ACTION

To download free copies of the following exercises go to *http://www.SetYourselfFree.com.au/relationships/exercises.htm*

### EXERCISE 4: INTIMACY - VALUES - FAMILY ROLES

The purpose and intention of this exercise is to:

- Clarify the adapted role/s you took on in your formative years that anchor you to past patterns of relating.
- Identify the false values and true values that are linked to the role/s so you can discern what you value in relating and relationships.
- Grieve losses and missed opportunities because of playing out your role/s and false values.

1. Name the predominant role you took on in your formative years. Specifically, how did that role give value to you and your family? If you adopted more than one role in your formative years, then answer the above questions for each role.

   _____

   _____

2. What have you missed out on because of this role?

   _____

   _____

3. How have you repeated this pattern in your adult relationships?
   _____
   _____

4. What has this cost you regarding intimacy?
   _____
   _____

5. What is your personal value within the role that you deeply honor as part of your code of ethics?
   _____
   _____

6. Is this a true value for you? Perhaps you adopted the value because it came along with your role?
   _____
   _____

7. Is there something else that is trying to emerge from you that is an expression of your identity?
   _____
   _____

8. Consider your primary or intimate relationships. Do you each have adapted roles that either causes conflict or complement each other? Write a brief summary of what you realize about this dynamic and what you would like to change about the way you are relating.
   _____
   _____

## ♡ EXERCISE 5: ASSESSING YOUR FEELINGS

As you read the information on feelings, what primary feeling(s) or awareness came up for you? Now, focus on the following questions, be as specific as you can; try not to complicate your thought process; often what first comes to mind is what you need to work with.

**In what specific relationships (past or present) are your feelings, or the lack of them, causing you issues or problems today?**

| RELATIONSHIPS | FEELINGS |
| --- | --- |
| *(consider family, personal, romantic, authority figures, business associates, co-workers)* | *(consider feelings such as anger, joy, pain, loneliness, fear, hurting, guilt, lust, shame)* |
|  |  |
|  |  |
|  |  |

## ♡ EXERCISE 6: ASSESSING YOUR BELIEFS

Consider your previous responses to your relationships and associated feelings. Now identify the limiting or negative beliefs that are associated with past or present relationships. Be as specific as you can; try not to complicate your thought process. Often what first comes to mind is what you need to work with.

**What limiting or negative beliefs are you able to identify that are blocking you from achieving healthy and happy relationships?**

| IDENTIFIED PROBLEMATIC FEELINGS AND RELATIONSHIPS | IDENTIFIED BELIEFS |
|---|---|
| | *Hopeless:* I have the ability/skills, but I just can't do it |
| | *Helpless:* I just don't have the ability/skills to do it |
| | *Worthless:* I don't deserve this because of something I did or didn't do |
| | |
| | |
| | |

CHAPTER 2: ANCHORS AWAY

## ♡ EXERCISE 7: ASSESSING YOUR BEHAVIORS

Consider your previous responses to your relationships, associated feelings and beliefs. Now, focus on the following questions; be as specific as you can, try not to complicate your thought process. Often what first comes to mind is what you need to work with.

### What behavior/s do you engage in or do that is/are:

| DISTRACTING | DESTRUCTIVE | ADDICTIVE |
|---|---|---|
| *Consider behaviors/ activities such as procrastination, always being busy, use of technology such as email, mobile phones, video games, TV; anything that takes you off focus from your needs, wants and desires)* | • *Fantasizing*<br>• *Mental obsession*<br>• *Causing hurt or harm to another or self*<br>• *Can be conscious or unconscious (i.e. withdrawing, withholding, shouting; any emotional, physical or verbal abuse, etc.)* | *May be a combination of distracting and destructive; are progressive and get worse over time. (i.e. any drug, alcohol, gambling, food, work or addiction, overly dependent, counter-dependent, sex or relationship intensity, sex, or relationship avoidance etc.)* |
|  |  |  |
|  |  |  |

## ♡ EXERCISE 8: BREAKING PATTERNS

The following is a simple, yet effective four-step process to break reactive behavior patterns.

1. When you feel triggered, reactive and find yourself repeating a behavior or pattern you don't wish to be enslaved to - STOP! Firstly, feel the feelings generated from this belief or message. Breathe deeply into the feelings and let yourself feel them. This allows you to 'free up' from the control these feelings have over you and to create the space to identify the negative message that is driving your reaction.

2. Secondly, identify a message or belief you carry which is driving this pattern of unwanted behavior. Get specific about what it is, getting any support you need to help you gain clarity.

3. Create an affirmation/new belief that states the integrity of the situation. Then say it out loud when you are feeling the undesirable feelings. For example, 'This is more about my mother's (father's, teacher's etc.) reality than it is about mine.' Or, 'This is more about my history than it is about what is happening right now.' Repeating the affirmation when you feel familiar feelings, continues to help you to disengage from the negative message/belief.

4. Take a deliberate action to interrupt the pattern. You don't have to get too concerned about taking the most appropriate (or 'right') action. It's more important for you to DO SOMETHING DIFFERENT - ANYTHING DIFFERENT will interrupt the pattern! Remember- even just get up from the couch!

It's also important not to analyze this too much. It's simple.

1. You stop lying to yourself, buying negative beliefs.
2. You gain control over your feelings by *embracing* them (simply allowing them to move, feeling them and breathing them through your body).
3. You speak your word - state the truth about the situation.
4. You rework your neurology by getting into action and doing something different.

Use the process for breaking a pattern whenever you feel triggered, and see that effective change can be simple.

# CHAPTER 3
# THE ROMANCE TRANCE

*The breezes at dawn have secrets to tell*
*Don't go back to sleep.*
*You must ask for what you really want*
*Don't go back to sleep.*
*People are going back and forth*
*Across the threshold*
*Where the two worlds meet*
*The door is round and open*
*Don't go back to sleep.*

Rumi

*'Keep your eyes on the pendulum, as you listen to the sound of my voice and you will soon fall deeply asleep. And once you are deeply asleep, you will do everything I tell you to do.'* Thanks to horror movies, you can probably picture a seedy looking hypnotist about to send his poor victim off to murder someone or rob the local bank.

## CHAPTER 3: THE ROMANCE TRANCE

There are many myths and fallacies about trance. Generally they induce fear of being controlled or manipulated to do something you don't want to do. That's exactly what happens when you get caught in what I call 'the romance trance'. You lose control and end up doing things that go against your values.

Like the swinging pendulum, we sometimes swing back and forth between life's polarities. Is it black or white? Is it good or bad? It depends. It can be great if we are fascinated with an opposite and not so great if we are power struggling with one. The 'romance trance' incorporates many diverse behaviors. What they all have in common is they induce or trigger patterns of automatic behaviors (trance) - usually 'swinging' behaviors that initially feel delightfully dizzy and after some time make us feel seasick! The challenge is to learn to dance between the polarities, while staying true to you.

Before we explore 'negative' trance, let's look at the other side of the polarity. Milton Erickson, the 'father of hypnotherapy' defines trance as a *'specialist learning state for change to occur'*. Trance doesn't happen because someone does something to you. Trance happens because you live. Let me explain.

Transcendent states include going beyond the 'normal self' (e.g. 'in the flow'; 'in the zone'; prayer; meditation; scientific breakthroughs; intense activities; rituals; etc.). These are the types of trance that let us take more control of our lives and make the breakthroughs and changes we want to make.

A trance can be triggered in many ways. Common trance triggers are:

### WHENEVER OUR IDENTITY IS DISRUPTED OR DESTABILIZED

Identity is basically the distinction of self - who am I? Represented in many modalities: thoughts, feelings, histories, images, physical places, our identity is the basis for navigating our world and our self. Multiple levels in which we organize identity are world, culture, family, relationship and individual. The good news about identity is that it continuously moves through cycles of death and rebirth.

## TRAUMA

Trauma can be experienced as any upset, disturbance, ordeal, suffering, pain or distress that causes emotional shock that may have long-lasting psychological effects.

## LIFE CHANGES AND DEVELOPMENTAL TRANSITIONS

Moving, changing schools, graduation/leaving school, puberty, leaving home, getting married, getting divorced, having a baby, the kids leaving the nest, health challenges, menopause, career changes, death of a loved one and retirement (not necessarily in this order) are examples of these type of changes and transitions.

## INTENTIONAL TRANCE

Hypnotherapy, counseling, self-hypnosis, prayer, meditation, accelerated learning and a multitude of other types of change work are some examples of people intentionally inducing trance. *Remember, lasting change happens on the neurological level, not the logical level.* These types of trance call for intentional action - doing something - perhaps doing something differently.

As you can see, trance happens because we live. It can be positive or negative, a conscious or unconscious choice. My question to you is, 'How are you choosing to dance in the relationship trances of life?'.

# ARE YOU SWINGING OR DANCING BETWEEN POLARITIES?

Polarities are not really the problem. Different views and healthy debates provide stimulation in relationships and offer solutions to problems one can have on their own. So what makes us 'swing' back and forth so much that we feel seasick?

Problems start when buried fear and/or shame get triggered, which affects our behaviors and the way we relate, especially the behaviors we witnessed from our parents or other significant adults during our formative years. Once the shine of the 'attraction stage' of a relationship starts to tarnish, we have an opportunity to get closer to someone in a more realistic way. This is a first step towards intimacy - and it will cause any unresolved fears and/or beliefs of inadequacy or worthlessness to surface. These buried feelings of fear or shame cause us to 'swing', often in extremes, between our polarities for no apparent reason. This swinging pendulum induces trance-like behavior in relationships - generally the behaviors that let us escape from intimacy.

What's really happening is our self-defense mechanisms are unconsciously distracting us from our buried, unpleasant feelings until we spin out and need a break. This way, no one can get close enough to discover all our 'bad' characteristics. Swinging between polarities is distracting behavior that creates confusion and conflict in relationships, causing couples to want to distance themselves from each other and even break up. If this behavior pattern is not interrupted, it can eventually progress to being addictive - whether you remain in the same relationship or move on to another.

When we are not swinging, we have the opportunity to 'dance' between the polarities. Dancing with a partner requires a balance of precision and letting go. Our higher self emerges from the integration of holding opposites, or what is known in eastern philosophies as 'the third law'. The gift of 'opposites attracting' is the opportunity to evolve and become more unlimited, while you're enjoying the dance or romance.

Diagram 6 shows some common polarities that surface in relationships. Neither side is good or bad. Imagine the pendulum in the center, motorized by fear and shame, swinging back and forth with no solution. If one swung *too* far to one side, the experience could be negative.

SET YOURSELF FREE IN RELATIONSHIPS

Diagram 7 shows an evolved experience when couples integrate both sides of the pendulum (what I call dancing between the polarities), creating healthier more balanced relating as illustrated in the center.

SWINGING IN POLARITIES
DIAGRAM 6
**Fear and shame induces trance (Swinging)**

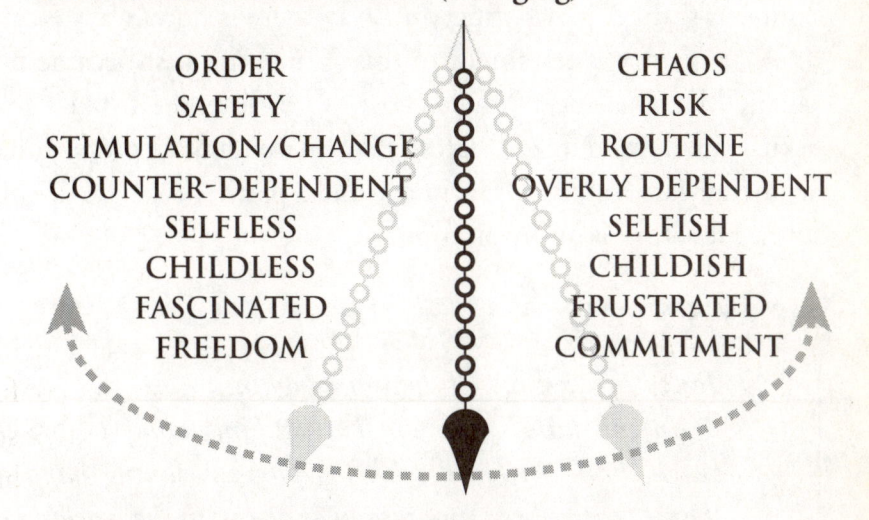

| | |
|---|---|
| ORDER | CHAOS |
| SAFETY | RISK |
| STIMULATION/CHANGE | ROUTINE |
| COUNTER-DEPENDENT | OVERLY DEPENDENT |
| SELFLESS | SELFISH |
| CHILDLESS | CHILDISH |
| FASCINATED | FRUSTRATED |
| FREEDOM | COMMITMENT |

DANCING BETWEEN THE POLARITIES
DIAGRAM 7

| | | |
|---|---|---|
| ORDER | **EVOLUTION** | CHAOS |
| SAFETY | **BUILDING RESERVES** | RISK |
| STIMULATION/ CHANGE | **BALANCE LIVING** | ROUTINE |
| COUNTER DEPENDENCE | **INTERDEPENCE** | OVERLY DEPENDENT |
| SELFLESS | **SELFING** | SELFISH |
| CHILDLESS | **CHILDLIKE** | CHILDISH |
| FASCINATED | **CURIOUS** | FRUSTRATED |
| FREEDOM | **INTIMACY** | COMMITMENT |

63

Have you longed for intimacy; more time and attention from your partner; good companionship and a satisfying sex life? Are you tired of your partner nagging, criticizing, or 'needing' something from you that you can't or won't give?

Whether you are in a miserable, dissatisfying relationship or you're single and don't want to be, the good news is: you really *can* create happy, healthy and fulfilling relationships. Charting the course is simple. Navigating your way there is not always easy!

Mary's story is testament to this. When she first became my client, Mary had been single most of her life. She'd had a few sexual affairs and fewer dates. Like many single, professional women, Mary longed for intimacy and a partner to share her life with. Her story is an inspiration.

## MARY'S STORY

*Today I found myself dreaming again.*

*In this familiar dream I'm walking along a glorious beach, hand in hand with my partner, feeling happier than I've ever been and totally at one with the world and myself. I know that I can have anything my heart and mind wants, and I'm tingling with the joy of being alive. Then, the shock of my true reality hits when I wake to find myself alone, with my doubts and fears, wondering how and when things will ever change.*

*Today, however, was different. This time I realized I was already awake, and the dream had become a reality. I found myself thinking back on my journey to this place.*

*My name is Mary and I grew up in a seemingly ordinary and normal middle class family. My Dad had a nine-to-five, Monday-to-Friday office job and hid behind the papers at night. Mom was a secretary, who stopped work when she married, had me, and five years later, my little brother Charlie. We lived in a suburban house with our cat, and had vacations every year. We didn't have a lavish lifestyle, but it was a comfortable one.*

*I adopted the family roles of 'surrogate spouse' and 'caretaker', always listening to my mother's complaints (usually about my Dad), trying to 'fix' her problems, and never holding an opinion or expressing an emotion contrary to that of hers. (If I did, I was quickly told that I was 'wrong' to think or feel that way.) I did this so well and for so many years, that I eventually lost touch with what I really felt or thought most of the time. Is it any wonder that I became a lawyer to prove myself in the world, yet, hiding the fact I felt terribly inadequate in my personal relationships - especially my love life?*

*I continued these roles of 'caretaker' and 'surrogate spouse' in my personal relationships, and to some extent in my work as a lawyer with Legal Aid. Often I would find myself with men who had lots of problems, who would put me down or try to control me. I found it increasingly impossible to be relaxed and confident, and wore myself out trying to guess what I 'should' be thinking, feeling or doing to win others approval. In the relationship department, what I felt, what I thought, and what I wanted, were a mystery to me. Relationships were either short-lived or non-existent. At the ripe old of age of 36, I realized I was more comfortable and probably better off on my own.*

*Just when I was about to give up, someone gave me the book '**Set Yourself Free**', by Shirley Smith and invited me to one of her lectures on relationships. Although I really didn't want to be seen at a lecture on relationships, it was my loneliness, frustration and, yes, desperation that led me to go. Besides, everything else I had tried hadn't worked - and believe me, I'd read many books, attended other courses and even saw a couple of counselors.*

*Although I didn't relate to the part of the lecture that talked about addictive dynamics, it was via this path that I finally made the breakthroughs I had wanted so much. I started to identify some of the patterns that had developed in my life that were holding me back from being truly myself and from having long-term intimacy with a man.*

*By participating in different programs and doing some life-changing exercises (like the ones in this book) I started to become alive again, feeling the full depth and breadth of my feelings that had been buried and frozen for so long. Anger was an unacceptable emotion in our home, and it was a long time before I could unleash it onto innocent and uncomplaining pillows and mattresses. The relief that afforded me in easing various chronic bodily aches and pains was astonishing. There were times when I had to summon up more courage than had I ever dreamt I had, to face and embrace crippling fear and shame. Without the education, exercises and emotional support of the programs I did with Shirley, I don't believe I could have done it.*

*There were many wonderful surprises along the way, such as how quickly I could release deep grief and be joyous and light-hearted minutes later. I discovered a sense of humor that had been hidden, as it was my brother who had been considered the funny one ('mascot') of the family. My playful, creative aspects began to blossom when released from their old bonds of shame and doubt. At the end of it, I found a new and wonderful 'me' and have felt comfortable with anyone in any situation ever since.*

*As a 'caretaker' I had only felt secure when in 'control' (although I learned that's always an illusion), so letting go and trusting the process was sometimes difficult and scary. One of the big changes was that I started taking more risks, having always played it safe before. I spoke up more boldly, ventured more daringly, dressed more sensuously, and played more frivolously. I got involved with a couple of men that still weren't 'right', but sensed it sooner and left before pain and drama ensued.*

*Then I met my current partner. From our first meeting there was an openness, honesty, and ease between us. We have been able to develop an intimacy that I used to dream about, through sharing our feelings (especially the so-called 'bad' ones that our society tends to shy away from - anger, fear, shame, pain) and being willing to really hear each other, even when it was uncomfortable to do so. I have had to apply many of the skills I learned in those programs, especially refraining from trying to control or 'fix' my partner, which at times takes a tremendous effort and support from others.*

*By reducing caretaking at work, I've actually been more effective at assisting my clients, and less drained. I have a better relationship with my parents, and can accept them for who they are, and can be my true self in their presence. I've learned how to communicate appropriately in my inner personal relationships and I'm more willing to confront others when there is a conflict between us, and can more readily hear others when they are upset with me.*

*The mask I used to wear, and the wall around my heart, have melted away to allow the real me to be seen, my true voice to be heard, and my soul to sing. My dream of someday becoming a radiant bride came true this year, and I never would have believed it was all an inside job!*

Mary has her dream relationship because she was willing to 'wake up' to herself, 'clean up' her past and 'skill up' to learn how to dance in rhythm with her partner.

There is another relationship dance that won't get you the wonderful results Mary got. You need to beware of this one. It's a swirling dance that spins people out - often ending in disaster!

## CO-ADDICTED RELATIONSHIPS

Co-addicted relationships are a painful and confusing aspect of the 'romance trance'. In the next part of this chapter I want to educate you about the dynamics of co-addictive relationships, so you can safely eliminate personal defenses and break the denial that keeps you trapped in frustration, preventing you from creating intimacy.

When examining couples' interactions, especially if one or both are either overly dependent or counter-dependent, I have found that they can easily become hooked on an addictive pattern of relating. I call this pattern of relating *'the co-addictive love dance'*.

When couples come in for counseling, the scenario usually goes like this: one partner appears to be more needy and desperate (the puppy-dog one), while the other seems to have things under control. Most would identify the 'needy one' as the one with significant problems. Another example could be that one partner has a problem with an addiction. The focus goes on the 'addict' as if fixing them will fix the relationship. Counseling couples for several years has shown me that *both* partners are equally involved in the problem.

Neediness or needlessness (as I've illustrated in chapter one) is a fundamental cause for addictive dances to occur between two people. Although co-addictive dynamics play out in all different types of relationships, it is usually the romantic/spousal ones where the most intense pain is felt. Why? Because these relationships trigger the deepest unresolved childhood issues of abandonment and engulfment, which we will explore deeper in Chapter 4.

Symptoms of painful love relationships are the most popular reason counselors and self-help book publishers are in business. I can't tell you the hundreds of times that I have asked an audience to raise their hand if they have tried marriage/couple counseling and to put their hand down if it worked. You guessed it. The only thing that drops is their face!

I believe this is because many couples are engaged in an intense addictive pattern they don't understand. This can be played out as an emotional rollercoaster ride or can be devastatingly disappointing when the relationship goes flat and feels empty. Either way, you become exhausted trying to make the relationship work or disillusioned when you can't.

Because of these dynamics, marriage/couple counseling is ineffective for co-addicts if treatment for addictive behavior or personal foundation work is not sought first.

Having healthy, happy relationships takes work. There are no shortcuts to romantic nirvana. There's no 'quick fix' to fill that empty feeling inside of you. If unresolved issues from your formative years are ignored, it almost always progresses to some form of addictive relationship pattern, especially in sexual, romantic or spousal relationships.

The more an individual experiences rejection or deprivation in their formative years, the more a person seeks security and a sense of wholeness (to feel the perceived hole inside) in their love relationships. Although these relationships are initially euphoric, they eventually develop into an addictive attachment. This pattern of coupling can only be interrupted when individuals focus on their own personal development. They must be willing to confront themselves first - their core negative beliefs; their buried feelings and the un-useful behaviors that keep them from moving towards relationships that are mutually enriching.

Your relationships are not the source of your problems. The 'missing bricks' in your personal foundation from unmet childhood needs and *the dysfunction in your parents' relationship* is the foundational problem. As you learned in Chapter 1, without a strong personal foundation, having a healthy, happy relationship is impossible. Co-addictive relationships are merely 'process addictions' that distract you from the intolerable reality of unresolved pain, anxiety and emptiness left over from childhood.

So if you have skimmed the earlier chapters and you are serious about wanting a healthy, intimate relationship, please go back and do the exercises in the first two chapters, as well as the ones in the rest of this book. The exercises will help you get clear, be more honest, and give you the ability to discern so you can make better choices.

## WHAT IS LOVE?

Before I define the co-addictive pattern of lovers, I'd like to give you my understanding of what love is. Love is about unconditional positive regard. When you love someone, you are able to honor and respect him or her as they go through their process in life. Your happiness and fulfillment do not depend on the mood that they're in. As long as they are not abusing or offending you, you can allow them to be angry, happy, sad or afraid, without the need to make them feel better. Love does not demand that you take away another's feelings ('Don't cry, it'll be alright' etc.) or fix their problems.

Think of love as an energy of balance and definition. Love is the energy that holds things in place. It is the grand definer of separateness and the grand binder of closeness. In the context of relationship, love defines how close to or how far apart from others we wish to be. When we can define our relationships clearly and without judgment, we will experience balance and harmony in them. For example, when I have a relationship with a client, I do not have the same expectations of them as I would have of a close friend or a lover. Similarly, I would not expect my lover to take care of me in a paternal way.

Kahil Gibran in *The Prophet* wrote one of the most beautiful and clear expressions of love I have ever read. The following extract represents, for me, the ideal way to relate lovingly in relationships.

*Love one another, but make not a bond of love:*
*Let it rather be a moving sea between the shores of your souls.*
*Fill each other's cup but drink not from one cup.*
*Give one another of your bread but eat not from the same loaf.*
*Sing and dance together and be joyous, but let each one of you be alone,*
*Even as the string of a lute are alone though they quiver with the same music.*
*Give your hearts, but not into each other's keeping.*
*For only the hand of Life can contain your hearts.*
*And stand together, yet not too near together:*
*For the pillars of the temple stand apart,*
*And the oak tree and the cypress grow not in each other's shadow.*

So why is there so much confusion about love today? And why don't we know how to love? The answer is ... we were never taught how. We learn by observation. From the cradle to the grave, we observe love as pain, guilt, martyrdom, self-denial, sacrificing, suffering, being used and sometimes even denying our own existence. Let's look at our role models for love relationships.

The movies often promise us a 'magical' kind of love; our churches tell us how we 'should' love others and often, behind closed doors, we experience horrendous examples of 'love' within our families. No wonder we're confused.

Think of the lyrics of the popular songs we grow up hearing and singing. Nearly all of them are about love and the great majorities have negative or painful messages about the nature of love.

'Nothing you can say can tear me away from my guy; nothing you can do cause I'm stuck like glue to my guy'

'Can't get you out of my head'

'I don't want to be alone. Help me make it through the night'

'If you leave me now, you'll take away the very heart of me'

CHAPTER 3: THE ROMANCE TRANCE

'I can't live, if living is without you'

'All I know is I'm lost without you'.

## YOU MIGHT AS WELL FACE IT – YOU'RE ADDICTED TO LOVE

This is a common yet painful refrain in our society today. Like any addiction, co-addictive relationships can reach chronic or fatal proportions if left untreated. Critics and public alike regarded the movie 'Fatal Attraction' as an extreme case, concocted by scriptwriters to achieve celluloid sensationalism. I will stick my neck out here and say that I believe that the love-addicted and pathologically violent behavior of Glenn Close's character is not as rare as we would like to believe. A client of mine who used to be in the police force told me a high percentage of the cases of homicide and suicide were due to these types of relationships. The prisons are full of untreated love addicts whose behavior escalated to criminal violence – usually unplanned.

Pia Mellody in her groundbreaking book *Facing Love Addiction* defines a love addict as 'someone assigning too much time, attention and value above themselves to any person they're in a relationship with. This is coupled with *unrealistic expectations* for unconditional, positive regard'.

Issues of neglect and abandonment set up these relationships. Co-addicts have an inordinate need to be loved and parented and tend to marry people who have their own parents' worst traits. Against all rational odds, they are attracted to partners who will abandon them. They will react to or re-enact their unresolved childhood issues of neglect and abandonment. Co-addicts see a potential partner through their own distorted reality; they make up a fantasy about the other person (have unrealistic expectations) and then they get angry and/or disappointed when the fantasy (romance) wears off.

Co-addicts' greatest fears are that of abandonment, engulfment, being controlled or intimacy. Addictive relationships take the place of true intimacy. They are loaded with lots of drama, game-playing and high intensity. The intensity of a co-addicted relationship is directly related to the degree that one's needs were unmet in childhood. Addictive lovers yearn to feel closeness, so they often connect through the intensity of anger and sex (fighting and making up). This pseudo-intimacy that co- addicts use is actually a wall of protection (isolation) against the possibility of experiencing hurt and disappointment. When you have true intimacy, you are vulnerable and open - to pain and disappointment, as well as to positive, euphoric feelings.

All types of relationship addiction are processes that take away intolerable reality. Because of that, such a process becomes the highest priority in a person's life, taking away time and attention from other priorities.

If I am feeling worthless, not good enough, incomplete, empty, lonely, needy or afraid to be alone (because of my own childhood issues of abandonment), I'd call that a pretty intolerable reality. In this instance, I would strive to distract myself by focusing on another, rather than face my own pain. I would want to meet their needs in order to become valuable to them, so that they wouldn't leave me and I wouldn't have to be alone (to face my emptiness).

The following checklist of attitudes and beliefs will help you to identify if you are in a co-addicted relationship:

1. My good feelings about who I am stem from being liked by you.

2. My good feelings about who I am stem from receiving approval from you.

3. Your struggle affects my serenity; my mental attention focuses on solving your problems or relieving your pain.

4. My mental attention is focused on pleasing you.

5. My mental attention is focused on protecting you.

6. My mental attention is focused on manipulating or controlling you. In other words: 'Do it my way'.
7. My self-esteem is bolstered by solving your problems.
8. My self-esteem is bolstered by relieving your pain.
9. My own hobbies and interests are put aside; my time is spent sharing your interests and hobbies.
10. Your clothing and personal appearance are dictated by my desires, as I feel you are a reflection of me.
11. Your behavior is dictated by my desires, as I feel you are a reflection of me.
12. I am not aware of how I feel, I'm aware of how you feel.
13. I am not aware of what I want. I ask what you want. Or I am not aware of what you want and I assume what you want.
14. The personal dreams I have for my future are linked to you.
15. My fear of rejection determines what I say or do.
16. My fear of your anger determines what I say or do.
17. I use giving as a way of feeling safe in our relationship.
18. My social circle diminishes as I involve myself with you.
19. I value your opinion and way of doing things more than my own.
20. The quality of my life is in relation to the quality of yours.

## THE CO-ADDICTIVE LOVE DANCE

'The 'co-addictive love dance' is even more destructive and exhausting than 'swinging in polarities'. This dance also goes back and forth, but is usually more intense - like a tango! Couples often mistake the intensity for intimacy or 'true love.'

When people keep dancing this dance, it creates an addictive cycle that is like a marathon dance contest, where people start dropping one by one. As you may already know, in this 'contest' the winners are really the losers! They tango back and forth between the fear of abandonment and the fear of being engulfed or controlled - and they both fear intimacy but don't know it.

There are basically two types of dance partners. On the surface, one appears to be the leader and the other the follower, so I have chosen those names to identify the two types. As you learn about this dance, keep in mind the power of paradoxes and the potency of opposites attracting. Understanding how these two principles play out in the dance is crucial to ending it.

The apparent *'leader'* is one who has a surface fear of being controlled or engulfed. Some examples of engulfment are being smothered; excessive attention; being overly critical; someone in your face; being fixed up; too much instructions and nagging. The paradox for the leader is a deeper underlying fear of abandonment that the surface fear is covering up. The leader can be a commitment phobic appearing strong, needless and in control. They can present as either passionate (connects through seduction) or aloof (mysterious, which breeds fantasy) and are put on pedestals by their partners. Notice the leaders back is to the follower. This represents avoidant and distancing behavior, yet out of his deeper fear abandonment his eyes (focus) are on the follower. Leaders are attracted to neediness so they can feel 'better than' and not risk uncovering their bigger fear of abandonment. Leaders are attracted to the follower so they can feel 'better than' and not risk uncovering their bigger fear of abandonment - *if they need me, they'll never leave me.*

The apparent *'follower'* is one who has a surface fear of abandonment and rejection. The paradox for the follower is a deeper underlying fear of intimacy (being engulfed; controlled; exposed) that the surface fear is covering up. They fantasize about their partners and pedestalize them, loving the high they get from their 'larger-than-life' partner. The follower can be quite a caretaker, which serves two purposes: 1) their need to be needed so they won't be abandoned; and 2) their need to focus on, control or fix their

# CHAPTER 3: THE ROMANCE TRANCE

partner to keep a distance, stay in fantasy and prevent intimacy. Because followers have unrealistic expectations, they often become disappointed and/or angry. They are forever waiting for their partners to change, and become disillusioned when they don't.

The diagram below illustrates the co-addictive lovers.

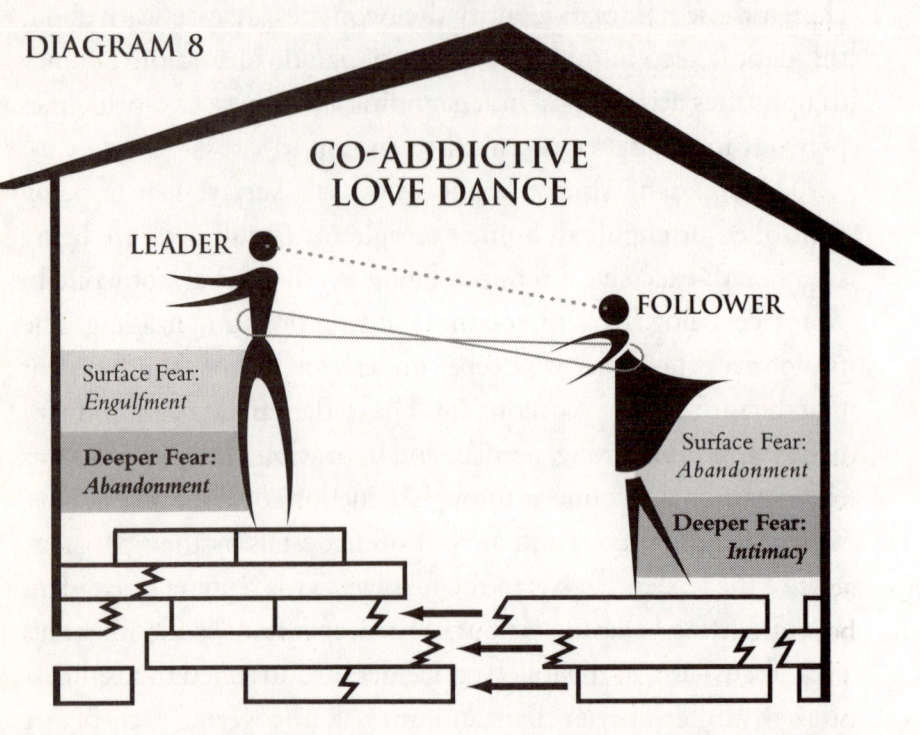

**DIAGRAM 8**

### CO-ADDICTIVE LOVE DANCE

**LEADER**
Surface Fear: *Engulfment*
Deeper Fear: *Abandonment*

**FOLLOWER**
Surface Fear: *Abandonment*
Deeper Fear: *Intimacy*

*Neither of these dance partners are leaders or followers.* They are caught in an addictive cycle that is an intense replacement for true intimacy, filling up the emptiness and loneliness in their relationship. Once the intensity is minimized, the partners often fear there is 'nothing between them'.

The emptiness triggers fear, loneliness and abandonment pain, causing the partners to unconsciously find ways to reconnect through intensity. This is often played out through sex, fighting or 'deep-and-meaningfuls'. Because it is too personally threatening, these partners don't create a healthy connection in their most important relationships, they stay forever stuck, dancing the same dance - feeling exhausted and disillusioned.

When I present this lecture in my *Set Yourself Free* programs, participants often relate to playing out the role of both follower and leader and ask if this is possible. The answer is yes! Sometimes we switch positions in our next relationship to protect ourselves from the pain we've experienced as a *follower or leader* in a former relationship. Some couples who stay together for many years switch positions in the later years of their relationship - like a role reversal.

The addictive love dance is not only reserved for romantic lovers. Many mothers and daughters; mothers and sons; fathers and daughters; fathers and sons - or in fact, any two people (friends, employees, employers etc.) can dance this dance!

## ENMESHMENT

Co-addicts have two choices in the way they relate to others - one is isolation and the other is intense, painful involvement (enmeshment). Generally, they vacillate between the two patterns.

Enmeshment is often mistaken for intimacy, when in fact it actually prevents it. When two people are enmeshed, they have no boundaries. They don't know where one ends and the other begins. This may be Hollywood's formula for true love and happiness, but in real life it produces a state of chaos and engulfment. When we are fused with another, we become con-fused!

## ESCAPES FROM INTIMACY

I use 'co-addictive relationships' as a general term to cover many types of addictive relationships because both parties are addictively dependent on each other, as well as the relationship. You can be co-addicted to any person - not only to romantic partners. It can be with your children, parents, friends, counselor, boss, sports coach, sponsor (in 12-step programs), minister, priest, rabbi, movie and pop stars, famous people (think of the international charisma of the late John F. Kennedy or Diana, Princess of Wales) or any authority figure.

CHAPTER 3: THE ROMANCE TRANCE

However, in this section I intend to focus on romantic, sexual, spousal types of co-addicted relationships. The following information is a précis of the work presented in Anne Wilson Schaef's book *Escape From Intimacy*. Schaef breaks these process addictions into three categories: romance addiction, sex addiction and relationship addiction. She claims that although these types of relationships appear to create intimacy, they are actually escapes from intimacy.

When I first read this material, it made a great impact on me because of its relevance to attaining personal freedom. Years ago, most of my relationships were addictive entanglements and the pain of these led me to seek help. This is how I discovered more about *my* behavior, what my personal needs were and how I could go about fulfilling them instead of expecting a man to. I began to feel free to do as I wished for the first time in my life. This was a liberating experience, learning how to be alone with myself - and enjoying it.

## ROMANCE ADDICTION

Romance addicts are addicted to their own fantasies and illusions about romance. It is the scene, the setting, the perfect picture that matters to them and gives them the high they are after. *The sad thing about romance addicts is that in their quest to look good to the outside world, they miss the actual experience - the authentic exchange of feelings and intimacy.* They love to pose. For them, the superficial appearance is the basis of the relationship. Women are especially into telling others about it. It's very important that others know that they're loved and admired. 'He sent me flowers and he's taking me to a romantic restaurant' or 'She's such a hot babe. All my buddies will be eating their hearts out.'

Schaef says romance addicts are 'experts at instant intimacy'. They'll tell you about this close, intimate relationship, they've found in which they talk about everything, staying up until the wee hours. They insist they've found their soul mate and so on. When you ask them how long they've been together, their reply is in the vicinity of 'six weeks'. Real intimacy takes years to build. This 'romance escape' is really an enmeshed relationship with no boundaries, which merely gives the illusion of connection.

Romance addicts, particularly if they carried a 'lost child' role in their family of origin, can have fantasy relationships in their minds. Fantasy is a way to defend against loneliness. When someone in the office smiles or is friendly, a romance addict can magnify this over time and play it out as a relationship in their heads. Sometimes, there are several fantasy relationships being held prisoner in the mind of a romance addict - so much so that there is confusion about what is real and what is not.

Romance addicts don't even need to be in a relationship because another form or romance addiction is being addicted to the cause. These types of romance addicts are the crusaders, out leading the peace movement and saving the world. Romance addiction is often prevalent in religion, politics and war. There is quite a bit of romance addiction running in the current 'war on terrorism'.

When you're engaging in any addictive process, it gives you an immediate and false high, which wears off in due course. Meanwhile, it cuts you off from having the totally satisfying experience of what you truly desire. Sometimes you can be so out of touch with yourself that you can't even identify your deepest desires. And as long as you continue to fuel your romance addictions, you'll never find out what they are.

I am a recovering romance addict and the following is an example of an incident from my life. Although it doesn't involve another person, the addictive process effectively cut me off from having the experience I desired.

Several years ago I desired to embrace some of my fears and to feel a new level of trust and connection with my higher power.

## CHAPTER 3: THE ROMANCE TRANCE

A spiritual adviser suggested that I should go and be alone in the wilderness for at least seven days. For someone whose idea of a relaxing vacation was room service and going to a spa at a five-star resort, this presented quite a challenge. The picture of me alone, communing with nature, immediately brought up some fears, but also a stirring of excitement and anticipation.

When I began telling all my friends of my daring plans, they oohed and aahed with envy. My mother flew into a panic saying, 'You can't do something like that without a man going with you'. This made my adventure more appealing.

Off I went with all my camping gear (no books, radio, CDs or junk food to distract me) and set up camp in the wilds. My unconscious expectation was to have a grand, spiritual experience. Each morning I rose and planned out my day with great ceremony. As I set out along one of the isolated hiking trails, I fantasized about what adventure might happen to me and how, on my return to the city, I would relay this to my friends at dinner parties. By the end of the third day, I felt tight, tense and unable to relax or meditate. I felt cut off from any connection with nature - or anything, for that matter. I was afraid I was going to miss the experience I'd craved. So I prayed and asked my higher power to help me.

Shortly after this, as I sat quietly, it dawned on me that I was operating in the same manner as I did in the city. I was organized, with my list of chores. I constantly tidied my campsite, washed the dishes and imagined in advance each activity I was about to undertake. I didn't allow myself to just 'be' in the moment. I realized that nobody cared about what I was doing in the wilderness; they were too consumed with their own lives. If upon my return, they asked about my adventures, I saw that they would be doing this mostly out of courtesy. I was more intent on setting up the 'perfect' experience and 'looking good' to others than actually allowing the natural experience I desired to happen to me. I then sat down, took a deep breath and realized that I didn't have to do anything in particular. I was free to do whatever I wanted. I looked around and noticed what a beautiful, sunny, October day it was and decided that what I really wanted to do was just lie in the sun. So I did - and that's when I had the spiritual experience I'd been looking for.

What all of this taught me was that such precious experiences are internal and private and when we try to share them with others (the hallmark of a romance addict), they are somehow diminished.

I'm not suggesting that we should completely eliminate romance from our lives. It can be fun; it's a great form of adult play. However, the important thing is to acknowledge romance for what it is, rather than assigning unrealistic meaning to it. Romantic interludes are delightful, but they are not life's ultimate experience or the foundation to build a relationship on!

## SEX ADDICTION

This is the most 'personal' and hidden addiction in our society. Our sense of self starts with gender identification. Sex is a central part of one's self-image and we all have deep emotions about it.

Considering the negative attitudes, cultural myths, mixed messages (advertisers blatantly sell 'sex', not mouthwash, jeans and flash cars), lack of proper education and the highly charged emotions associated with sex, it is no surprise that much sexual behavior is hidden and furtive.

Sexual addiction is so integrated into our social structures, it has come to be regarded as normal. Most sexual addiction is set up by sexual abuse in childhood and carries a large component of shame. Children with sexually repressed parents are often carrying and acting out their parents' repressed lust.

Sexual addiction is an obsession and preoccupation with sex in which most things are defined sexually or by their sexuality;

and most perceptions and relationships are sexualized.

Having sex is a mood-altering experience that can be highly pleasurable. And this is fine. However, a sex addict will sexually act out or mentally obsess and fantasize about sex in order to avoid dealing with their uncomfortable feelings or their life in general.

Dr Patrick Carnes, in his breakthrough work on sexual addiction, *Out of The Shadows,* defines sexual addiction in three categories. According to Carnes, '*Level One* behaviors have in common general cultural acceptance ... but each can be devastating when done compulsively.' Such behaviors include masturbating, looking at pornography, patronizing prostitutes, going to strip shows. In a sexual relationship with a Level One sex addict, 'one partner sacrifices important parts of the total relationship in the service of sexual needs.'

*Level Two* sexually addictive behaviors are intrusive enough to warrant stiff legal actions. They include voyeurism, exhibitionism, making indecent telephone calls, making inappropriate sexual advances.

*Level Three* behaviors are generally more severe and more overtly illegal.

They include rape, incest, child molesting, sadomasochism and sexual torture. (There are a number of religious cults that incorporate sexual rituals and even sexual torture into their ceremonies).

Sexual anorexia is also a form of sexual addiction. The sexual anorexic is a person who is obsessed with sex ... but they're obsessed with avoiding it. A new client once told me that she had dealt with her sex addiction/promiscuity about five years previously because it was causing her so much pain. This client was a recovering alcoholic and I was quite interested to hear how she had dealt with her sex addiction. She told me she had been celibate for the previous five years. This woman was also in my office because she longed for a fulfilling, loving relationship with a man. She was in her mid-30s and desperately wanted to have children. I explained to her that her sexual anorexia was not the solution to her problem. Her decision to be celibate was not a choice, but rather a reaction based on her fear of trusting herself with her sexually addictive behavior.

A person may be sexually anorexic because during their upbringing they received a lot of shaming messages about their bodies and sex. Many religiously addicted parents convey to their children shaming messages about the harmful consequences of sex. (Whatever you repress, you will become obsessed with.)

Another form of sexual addiction is the addiction to sexual fantasy. This does not take the form of sexually acting out, rather these addicts sexually 'act in' - in their minds. These types avoid dealing with their pain and emotions by losing themselves in constant sexual fantasies and 'affairs of the heart'. This can also be done when parents sexualize their relationships with their children at the emotional and intellectual levels, although not actually having sex with them. A graphic example of this was related to me by one of my former clients. She told me how when she was a teenager her father approached her before Christmas, asking her to choose between a diamond ring and a sewing machine. He told her that she had first choice and he would give the remaining gift to her mother. This made her feel terribly guilty and ashamed.

There is a widely held misconception that sex addicts are perverted people. Often, sex addicts are married or in committed relationships and they use these partnerships to get their sexual fixes. Sex is the basis of their relationships and they are afraid to leave because they don't know where they would get their consistent supply. With the rising concern of AIDS, other STDs and all the talk about the need for safe sex, remaining in a 'safe', sexually addictive relationship becomes paramount for them.

Despite the dangers of illicit affairs, some sex addicts are still rampantly promiscuous. The line of reasoning frequently used to blame a wife for her husband's affairs is that if she had been more sexually available to him, he would not have had to resort to having affairs. There is little understanding that the husband's promiscuous behavior is often caused by an addiction, not by his wife. Just as alcoholics drown their emotional pain by drinking to excess, sex addicts medicate their emotional pain with the escape and relief they get through sexual affairs, pornography and compulsive masturbation.

When a romance addict and a sex addict pair up, their relationship will often escalate into violence. This is the source of the 'Fatal Attraction' syndrome.

## RELATIONSHIP ADDICTION

Schaef nominates three types of relationship addiction:

1. *Being addicted to having a relationship*

    The requirement here is to always be a couple, always be connected to someone. This relationship addict fears being alone and can only feel safe, secure and worthy when they are in a relationship. Their addiction is to the concept of a relationship. Their partner's values, personality and aspirations are not considered. This addict just wants someone to be in a relationship with him or her.

    This type of person has overlapping relationships. Usually, they won't relinquish their current relationship until they are sure they have someone else waiting in the wings.

2. *Being addicted while in a relationship*

    This person can be out of a relationship for long periods of time and feel quite comfortable about this. Yet when they enter into a new relationship, they immediately get hooked. They become needy and whining and start to slip in areas in their lives where previously they were taking care of themselves quite well. This syndrome is common among women in high-powered jobs. Such women are successful and independent and these qualities make them very appealing to men. Yet within 90 days in relationship with a man, they become lovesick lap dogs.

3. *Cling-clung addiction*

This type of relationship addict practises their relationship addiction on everyone they meet. Most of us have been around this type of person. These addicts have no boundaries, act intrusively and appear to be very needy, victim types. Usually they are adept at manipulating others to feel sorry for them.

Relationship addicts move from one relationship to another and they also have selective amnesia. In other words, they very quickly and conveniently forget the pain of their past relationships in order to maintain their relationship addiction. They are very controlling people, who believe they can make relationships happen by sheer force of their own will. Relationship addicts do not have relationships - THEY HAVE HOSTAGES!

## ARE YOU IN RITUAL OR ARE YOU IN RELATIONSHIP?

Schaef presents an excellent adaptation, in relationship terms, of Carnes' 'cycle of addiction'.

### Stage 1: Preoccupation

This is the obsession stage of the relationship. It has a trance-like, mood-altering facet to it. The person is totally absorbed in the relationship. The woman may talk about it incessantly to her friends. The man may be unable to concentrate on the job because he's fantasizing about his date with her that evening.

### Stage 2: Ritualization.

This is the behavioral process undertaken when establishing a relationship. For women it may take the form of dieting, exercising, having beauty treatments, a new hairstyle; for men, courtship may be ritualised, 'I should give her flowers and buy her dinner.' 'It will make her warm to me enough to have her invite me in for a drink and then ...'

**Stage 3: Compulsive relationship behavior**
This involves establishing as early as possible the status of the relationship, or as Schaef says; 'nailing down the relationship and holding on to it for dear life'. 'Are we committed?' 'Are we going to date others?' 'Are we monogamous?', or discussing marriage or getting married when the relationship is still in the 'attraction' stage.

**Stage 4: Despair**
This is when the addict realizes that the relationship isn't going to 'fix' them and they sink into the feeling of hopelessness and despair. In other words, 'the honeymoon is over'. At this point, they will either move on to another relationship or fixate on some problematic aspect of their current relationship in order to become preoccupied. And so the cycle starts over again.

The three primary forms of love addiction are well summed up by Schaef :

1. Romance addicts MOVE ON.
2. Sex addicts COME ON.
3. Relationship addicts HANG ON.

## TO OPEN A NEW DOOR ... CLOSE THE OLD ONE

The reason many of us don't have the types of relationships we want is that we haven't learned how to complete our past relationships. The most important relationships in our past that we need to complete are those with our mother, father and siblings. Total healing and freedom comes from completing our relationship with our family of origin. By the time we're adults, we usually have several other 'incomplete relationships' and we carry the wounds of them into our current relationships.

By completing a relationship, I don't necessarily mean finishing it. The process of completion lets you take pearls of wisdom and teaches you how to come to terms with the past so that you can close the door on it. This course of action allows many new doors to be opened.

Sometimes when we complete a past relationship, we say goodbye to the other person and go our separate ways. This seems a straightforward process, yet it's one that people seem to struggle with a lot. Why? Reasons people give include: 'I'll feel guilty', 'It'll hurt too much', 'I owe it to them to stay', 'It's easier to forget about it and just go on'.

It's also possible to create a new beginning in an ongoing relationship by completing the *past* relationship you shared with that person. By now you have probably identified some addictive patterns of relating you'd like to change. The exercises at the end of this chapter will help you do that. Once you 'complete' an addictive cycle, many doors to new possibilities begin to open for you. It's a process of *letting the old relationship die so a new one can be born.*

Couples in long-term relationships have the opportunity to go through many wonderful life stages together or, like my parents, they can stay addicted to power-struggle. Those open to change, healing and evolution may feel like they have been with several different partners during the course of their relationship, which keeps things stimulating and allows love to grow.

I once heard a very wise saying about this: 'My pain comes from leaving my fingers in doors that are closing'. If it seems there are no opportunities in your life either for new relationships or for improving the quality of your existing relationships, you might like to look at which doors you have your fingers in! Once you identify which doors (relationships) your fingers are stuck in and you're tired of the pain, you then can pull them out and close the door/s. When we complete the past in this way, we *release* it rather than *relive* it.

## TREATING CO-ADDICTIVE RELATIONSHIPS

I learned the following treatment model for healing addictive relationships while doing an intern program at The Meadows Treatment Center in Arizona in 1989 from Pia Mellody. Since that time I have worked with hundreds of people to heal addictive behaviors in their relationships with much success. I believe that uncovering the addictive patterns of relating and healing them lets people move forward in their lives and have satisfying love relationships.

If you have identified yourself as being a co-addict, your first step is to arrest the addiction. This will immediately put you into withdrawal. Withdrawal is a deep grieving and healing process that takes a few months to go through. It's very important to get support during this time from a professional or a self-help group that has members who have gone through this process. It is equally important to take good care of yourself during the withdrawal process. In Chapter 2, Anchors Away, the section called 'Good Grief' gives you steps for self-care. I suggest you reread it.

Although withdrawal can be intense and confusing, it is necessary to heal deep wounds and lets you build intimacy with yourself. In Al-Anon, a 12-step program for partners and family members of alcoholics, they have a saying that gives three simple steps to use to take you through the withdrawal process.

1. 'Get off their back' (learning detachment).

2. 'Get out of their way' (creating boundaries).

3. 'Turn and go on with your life' (rebuilding your personal foundation).

While you're in the withdrawal process, it is necessary to establish boundaries as soon as possible. This will help to stabilize the emotional fluctuations that make you feel like you're on a rollercoaster. Many love addicts have to begin their recovery by detaching and using what Pia calls a 'wall of pleasant'. A 'wall of pleasant' is smiling, being polite and mannerly and communicating on a surface level. This is not the time to share any profound realizations or deep feelings. This mode of behavior takes the toxic energy out of communicating with the people to whom you're addicted.

Rage, desolation, carried pain, fear and shame, as well as panic attacks, feelings of betrayal, jealousy and mental obsession are all commonly experienced during withdrawal from co-addicted relationships. In fact, withdrawal from this is the most emotionally painful withdrawal of any addiction (more painful even than heroin).

Understanding the various stages of withdrawal is important for two reasons. Most people have no idea of the intensity that accompanies withdrawal and think something is seriously wrong with them when they are in it. This causes extreme reactive behavior and leads to decisions made from desperation. Secondly, when you are educated about the process of withdrawal, you know what to expect and you also know *there's an end to it*.

The reason the pain of withdrawal is so overwhelming is that it stimulates deep abandonment pain, not only from the person you've been addicted to, but from childhood abandonment issues. Although this is an intensely painful process, it is one that will lead you to an experience of profound transformation as it allows a part of you which has been trying to surface for a long time, to do so. Going through withdrawal helps you become a whole person, to know and have an intimate relationship with yourself. Withdrawal holds the beginnings of your own personal healing and wholeness. And its end effect, which makes the process worthwhile, is that addictive sexual and emotional behavior, on a daily basis, stops.

## STAGES OF WITHDRAWAL

I tell a client that going through withdrawal is like going through 'the valley of the shadow of death'. At times it may feel like you're dying - and perhaps a part of the shadow-self is! Having said that, withdrawal has predictable stages and more importantly - when it's over - it's over! People tell me that they feel stronger, clearer and freer than they ever could imagine. Just as any difficult challenge, once it's over, they tell me they are glad they went through it. Below are the stages:

### Stage 1: Fear, pain and sometimes panic

This is usually triggered by rejection or abandonment from the one you're addicted to - even if you initiated the split. In this stage it is very common to feel totally overwhelmed or like you don't even want to get out of bed. People report having suicidal and/or homicidal thoughts. These are nothing more than desperate thoughts, trying to help us look for a way out of the pain. The way out of this, which gives lasting freedom, is to *go through it.* Don't get stuck wallowing in stage one - keep going!

### Stage 2: Obsession

This is where a co-addict starts mentally obsessing and fantasizing about a plan of action to get the other person back. Although most people don't realize it, mental obsession effectively mood-alters overwhelming emotions. This mental obsessing takes the co-addict out of their intense feelings and puts them into their heads, which relieves their panic and pain. This also installs a false sense of hope that everything can be ironed out with a quick solution.

### Stage 3: Compulsion

This is the stage where the co-addict acts out their obsession to get attention or a reaction out of the person they're addicted to. This stage usually carries lots of high drama and intensity, which gives the love addict relief for a short while. Because love addicts have a deep, underlying fear of intimacy, they learn to connect through intensity and are confused about the difference between the two.

Repeating stages 1, 2, and 3 of the withdrawal process keeps the addictive cycle going and keeps you stuck in misery. *The place to intervene is in the obsession stage.* It is okay for you to go ahead and obsess - only if you wait and don't act out a plan. Say to yourself: 'Who he/she is, is none of my business'. Once you've done this, the fear and panic will increase. Now is the time to use a mantra, insert a positive belief or pray. Doing this, will serve to calm you down and center you. Having a few new beliefs ready is a good idea. The exercise 'Breaking Patterns' at the end of Chapter 2, Anchors Away, will help prepare you.

Another thing you can do is to make an appointment to obsess at another time. For example, if you're at work and you can't stop thinking about your relationship, make a time and put it in your appointment book to totally indulge and obsess about it at, say 6 pm. You'll often find that if you do this, by 6pm it might not be such a big deal any more. You may even be able to see some humor in it. Once you stop obsessing:

- Ask for what you want from the other person.

- WAIT. Keep quiet and keep breathing.

- Pay attention to what you're actually getting. What can you take from the relationship?

- Accept 'no'. Learn how to meet your own needs.

If, after a while, you notice that you're not getting what you want from the relationship, you'll know it's time to move on. However, once you wait, keep quiet and notice what you get, you often find that you're getting a lot more than you may have noticed previously.

Once the intensity of withdrawal starts to subside, you're ready to write an inventory of your co-addictive behavior with more honesty and clarity. First, write about how you assign too much time, attention and value to the other person. Second, write about how you expect too much unconditional, positive regard from the other person. Third, write an inventory of how your partner seduces you and gets a rise out of you (which keeps you hooked in the intensity of the relationship). There is an exercise at the end of this chapter that will help you do this.

Once you've done this thoroughly, you'll get new insights into where you've gone wrong. Your new-found clarity lets you begin to decide on the proper course of action to help you to restore your self-confidence, create boundaries, meet your own needs and make more value-based choices.

Waking up from the romance trance is not something the majority of people are willing to do unless they are in a tremendous amount of pain or life gives them no other choice. You can take control of your life by choosing to be accountable for the quality of your relationships. The exercises below will help give you the inner strength to do this.

## ACCOUNTABLE ACTION

It can be helpful to have a support person to share these exercises with, especially someone who will not criticize you or try to solve your problems. If you share your responses with another, have the intent to heal, feel validated and move on. It can also be helpful to seek the support of a professional at this time, particularly someone who is trained to help people with addictive dynamics.

To download free copies of the following exercises go to *http://www.SetYourselfFree.com.au/relationships/exercises.htm*

### ♡ EXERCISE 9: COMPLETING RELATIONSHIPS PROCESS

This is a letter-writing process. Find a private place where you can be alone and allow yourself plenty of time. Select the person with whom you wish to complete your relationship. You will be writing six different letters to that person. These letters are not meant to be sent or even seen by anyone else (unless you're sharing them with a counselor or in a confidential group with the intent of healing).

First, set your intention to be complete. The power of your intention is the most important element in this process. Before you start writing, I suggest that you ask a Higher Power to help you to do this authentically and thoroughly, to the best of your ability.

**Letter Number 1:**
In this letter, you are to express all of your feelings of anger and hatred towards this person - no holds barred! Do not edit or censor what you write. Allow it to be a cathartic process and simply 'pour' your emotions onto the page.

**Letter Number 2:**
In this letter, you are to express your feelings of hurt and pain. Allow your emotions to flow. Many people cry and sometimes even sob. In your letter, include ways in which you felt betrayed, offended and violated.

**Letter Number 3:**
In this letter, communicate your fears about completing the relationship and your fears about relationships in general. For example, 'I'm afraid that I'll become bitter', 'I'm afraid I'll put up walls and never be able to trust again', 'I'm afraid I'll never achieve intimacy', 'I'm afraid I'll never be able to get you out of my mind', 'I'm afraid I can't change', 'I'm afraid you won't change', 'I'm afraid I'll see you with another lover', 'I'm afraid I'll run into you and get caught off guard' etc. Be as thorough as possible in listing your fears. By acknowledging them, you take a lot of the 'charge' out of them. Should any of these things occur in the future, you won't have such a strong emotional reaction. There is a process in *Set Yourself Free* called 'Embracing Fear' that is particularly useful to eliminate reactive behavior generated from fear. Go to *http://www.SetYourselfFree.com.au* to order.

**Letter Number 4:**
In this letter, you acknowledge and account for your own involvement and participation in the dysfunction or addictive pattern of the relationship. Acknowledge the bad choices you made, identify where you sold out in pursuit of instant gratification and where your thinking and feelings were distorted and how your behavior contributed negatively (eg. 'he introduced me to his mother, therefore he wants to marry me' or 'now that we're married, I don't have to be so particular about my appearance').

**Letter Number 5:**
In this letter, write what your needs, wants and desires are regarding the relationship - in other words, how you would like it to be. Obviously if it's someone with whom you intend to remain in contact, it is important to be very specific and to take time and care with this letter. Perhaps this person is someone you don't desire to have a friendship with, but whom you'd respond pleasantly to if your paths crossed. Then again, if it's someone you don't intend to see again, you might wish him or her peace and love on their path, but state that you wish no further contact with them.

**Letter Number 6:**
This is a letter of love and appreciation. In this letter, you look for the 'good purpose' of the relationship, as well as the knowledge and wisdom you gained from it. The intention in this letter is to complete the relationship, so that you finally can close the door on the past (accept and release it) and move forward to create a healthy relationship - either with or without them.

Don't underestimate the power of this simple process. Many clients report having experienced radical shifts and miracles in their lives as a direct result of this process. Sometimes the letter-writing process highlights the fact that there is something outstanding that needs to be communicated. If this is the case, you will now be clear to write another letter (and post it) that says what you really need to say, without being offensive or dumping on them.

## ♡ EXERCISE 10: TREATMENT FOR CO-ADDICTED RELATIONSHIPS

The following exercise will help you identify, heal and change co-addictive dynamics in your relationships.

**Part 1: Inventory**
The first step is to observe and inventory your addictive behavior patterns regarding issues of abandonment and engulfment.

1. Select either a relationship from your past or a current relationship that has caused you discomfort, confusion or intense pain.

2. Using either your dominant or non-dominant hand (or you may alternate) write about the following in journal form:

*Fear of engulfment (avoiding/withdrawing)*

Consider your past and present behaviors. Although the questions below are worded in the present tense, please also consider your past behaviors and answer accordingly. Example: did/do, were/are, was/is.

    a) How do you avoid:

- Spending time with

_____

- Paying attention to

_____

- Acknowledging and valuing the other person.

_____

    b) How do you perceive that you were 'better than' and/or more powerful than your partner?

_____

CHAPTER 3: THE ROMANCE TRANCE

c) Specifically, what thoughts or behaviors do you use to distance yourself from your partner and control the relationship.

_____

*Fear of abandonment (pedestalizing/caretaking)*

Consider your past and present behaviors. Although the questions overleaf are worded in the present tense, please also consider your past behaviors and answer accordingly. Example: did/do, were/are, was/is.

a) How do you assign:

_____

- too much time

_____

- too much attention

_____

- too much value to another before your own self-care.

_____

b) How do you think that you were 'less than' and/or less powerful than your partner?

_____

c) What thoughts or behaviors do you use to engulf your partner and control your relationship?

_____

3. What are some of your unrealistic expectations? In what specific ways do you expect too much unconditional positive regard? List them in bullet point form.

_____

4. Specifically, how do you polarize in your relationships?

   _____

5. In what specific ways is your behavior needy or needless?

   _____

6. How have you allowed another to seduce or influence you to do something you really did not want to do?

   _____

7. How have you seduced or influenced another to get your way?

   _____

8. How do you use drama, anger, making up and/or sex to create intensity and give you the illusion of being connected? (Be specific as possible.)

   _____

9. How are your behaviors taking away your choices and how is this affecting other areas of your life (i.e. career, parenting, friendships, physical vitality, spirituality, mental clarity, emotional well-being, sexuality)?

   _____

## PART 2: COMMITMENT TO CHANGE

Once you have decided to make changes, to build faith and trust in yourself, it is important to commit to changing only what you are willing to follow through on. It's better to select a couple of behaviors and focus on making change at a deep level rather than set yourself up to fail with too many changes at once.

1. The behaviors I am willing to change and work with now are:

   _____

2. The new steps I will take now are (generate at least three steps or different options for each desired change):

   _____

3. This is how I am going to support myself as I go through this process of change.

   _____

## ♡ EXERCISE 11: KEYS TO INTERDEPENDENCY

If you know you are overly dependent in certain areas of your life or if you know you are a completely dependent type, using the following keys is like opening up a treasure chest you've found in a shipwreck. Putting them into practice will assist you to become interdependent.

- The first thing to do is make a decision that you are capable of being independent and then sit down and write your own 'Declaration of Independence'. Combining your intention and writing makes a very powerful therapeutic tool. Begin to think of what you will allow and what you will not allow in your life and list the specific areas - career, your body, your partner, parents, children, finances, sex, and so on. In your declaration, spell out for yourself how you want to function in all relationships. Stay open to negotiation and co-operation, but eliminate any manipulation. Write it in the first person, for example, 'I, Shirley, in order to have more balance and freedom in my life, now declare ...'

- Talk to each person you feel psychologically dependent on in some way. When you do this, state your aim to function independently and explain how you feel when you do things out of a sense of sacrifice and obligation. You might wish to explain you'd like to have more intimacy in your relationship and that dependency destroys intimacy. (We usually give out of obligation because we have a hidden agenda - unconscious expectations or unspoken expectations). When you're honest about this type of behavior, you own your dependency - which then allows it to shift. This is an excellent strategy for getting started because others may not even be aware that you feel dependent.

- Experiment with how you handle the dominant people in your life. These are the people you have difficulty saying 'no' to. Try saying, 'No, I don't want to' without giving any reason, and test the other person's reaction. When you tell yourself you're doing this as an experiment, it will help you to start saying 'no' when you mean no and 'yes' when you mean yes. Giving people reasons is a way to keep you hooked on your dependency and is a waste of energy. Basically, we are all motivated by our needs, wants and desires - not reasons. We take action or refrain from taking action because we want to - period.

You're the one who will face the consequences of all your decisions and behavior as an adult, so you have the right to do what you want to do. Give yourself permission.

- Arrange a planning session with your dominant partner at a time when neither of you is feeling highly charged nor over-reactive, especially when you're not feeling threatened. During this session, state how you sometimes feel manipulated and submissive. Explain that you would like to agree on a non-verbal signal whenever you're feeling dependent on that person, but you don't want to discuss it at the time (e.g. tugging an ear or tapping two fingers on your heart).

- The moment you feel shoved around psychologically, stop and state how you feel. Then, even do something different to interrupt the pattern and act the way you'd like to behave. ('Fake-it-till you-make-it' is sometimes the only way that you can begin to change your dependency patterns.)

- Frequently remind yourself that your parents, spouses, friends, bosses, children and others will often disapprove of your behavior, but this has nothing to do with who you are. It is a given fact in any relationship that you will incur some disapproval. If you learn to expect this disapproval, then you won't be surprised by it. In this way, you can break free of many of the dependency ties that enslave you emotionally.

- By deliberately avoiding dominant people, you are still allowing yourself to be controlled by them if you experience emotional immobilization because of them. If it's too confronting to speak up, send a letter saying how you want your interactions to change.

- If you feel obligated to visit or spend time with certain people, ask yourself if you would want others to do the same with you simply because they felt required to do so. If this is the case, talk about it with them, explaining the concerns behind your obligated behavior.

- Make a firm decision to get out of your dependency role by doing volunteer work, reading, getting childcare, getting a job (even if you don't financially need one) because the remuneration of your own money in any creative way that you can devise is important to your independence.

- Recognize your desire and need for privacy and stop feeling as though you need to share everything you feel and experience with someone. You are a unique and special individual. If you think you must share everything, then you are without a choice, and of course, dependent.

# CHAPTER 4

# BREAKING THE FANTASY BOND

*It's not the traumas we suffer in childhood
that makes us emotionally ill,
but the inability to express the trauma.*

Alice Miller

The information presented in Chapter 3, 'The Romance Trance,' is not for the 'faint of heart'. In fact, most of my clients report feeling a bit sick once they've read it. This is a normal response because the information and exercises stir up buried feelings associated with issues of abandonment, engulfment, rejection and the fear of intimacy. These issues hold one's deepest fears and negative beliefs. You can't address them without feeling anxiety.

If you've identified some dependent behaviors or co-addictive patterns of relating in your current or past relationships, then you are probably trapped in the 'Fantasy Bond' - a condition that holds miserable, destructive and unsatisfying relationship patterns in place. To completely release co-addictive behaviors and create intimacy, you have to address the core of the problem - the unhealed wounds from childhood abandonment and engulfment issues - which requires deep emotional healing. To break free and heal

## CHAPTER 4: BREAKING THE FANTASY BOND

these wounds you need education, as well as structured support and guidance. This chapter will help you to do this.

Even if you are not presently in a co-addictive relationship or do not have a current partner, it is important to heal and resolve these issues because they will surface again, reeking havoc in your future relationships.

The healing process involves regressive work, grieving the unhealed wounds from your childhood, *as well as grieving your parents' unhealed wounds from their childhood that you may be carrying.* Often there is some mystique linked with regressive healing, so I'd like to explain what I mean by this and why regressive work is extremely important to interrupt patterns and heal intense emotions that drive behaviors we don't want.

The dictionary defines regression as 'returning to an earlier or less-developed way of behaving, usually less mature and less adaptive on the emotional and mental levels'. Regressive healing work involves deliberately becoming aware of buried childhood emotions and breaking up their intensity, because these emotions trigger destructive behaviors - particularly in our close relationships.

Feelings are not necessarily valid just because one has them. The therapeutic purpose of accepting and expressing feelings from our formative years is to help overcome societal prejudices against emotion and to release the stigma attached to feelings in childhood that parents and other adults considered unjustified.

To *embrace* a feeling is to be able to step aside from the child feeling expression and identify that the feeling is actually coming from a timeframe from the past that has nothing to do with the present. Feelings that have their source in childhood are valid, but not as an appropriate response to present-day situations.

Success in regressive healing work is attained when one can distinguish whether one's thoughts and feelings are occurring in response to past childhood events or whether they are truly a reasonable reaction to present circumstances. (The exercise at the end of this chapter, 'Embracing Abandonment or Engulfment' is a powerful healing exercise that will allow you to do this.)

## ABANDONMENT: THE ROOT OF DEPENDENCY

Abandonment includes being neglected, abused and enmeshed (enmeshed meaning entangled; trapped). The reason we have so much denial about this is that childhood abandonment exists in many forms beyond the average person's recognition and understanding. Before defining some of the various forms of childhood abandonment, there is something important that must be understood first ...

It takes many years for children to fully develop their intellect and their ability to reason. Their earliest way of thinking is through what John Bradshaw calls 'felt-thought'. Children gain understanding through their emotional reality. Although they don't logically understand it, a child can feel if others are angry, fearful, sad, guilty or especially if someone is not present and is cut off emotionally.

For children to grow, develop and mature, they have to be egocentric, putting a lot of focus on themselves. In their self-focused way of relating, children take everything personally, including when they are neglected or abandoned. Until they are about seven or eight (the age of reason), they lack the ability to understand this logically. If others, especially adults, are not present with them (neglecting or rejecting them), children feel like it is their fault. These factors become very important in understanding issues of abandonment and why children learn to build an internal world of fantasy to emotionally nourish themselves. This is their way of surviving.

There are three types of childhood abandonment: physical, emotional and abandonment through abuse.

## CHAPTER 4: BREAKING THE FANTASY BOND

## PHYSICAL ABANDONMENT

This is commonly understood as occurring when there is parental death, desertion, divorce, adoption, or a serious parental illness. In addition, children are abandoned when their parents don't give them their time - for whatever reasons. Remembering that a child can't reason and will take things personally; no matter what the circumstances are, a child senses that a parent gives his or her time to what they love. A child will actually feel worth less than their parents' time. We mistakenly ignore the consequences of this or deny the abandonment altogether because the many 'reasons' seem justified. Perhaps the parents are workaholics, busy or always on the go. Two-income families or single-parent families are common these days, so parents are often pressed for time. Or in large families, with several children, the bottom line is that the parents cannot make enough time for each child.

Children, being egocentric, will always interpret these types of events in that light. If Mom or Dad is not present for whatever reason, a child interprets that they are the reason. He or she must have done something bad or maybe they are just plain bad. This is why they have been abandoned.

Sometimes the physical abandonment is overt and obvious. When we look back on it as adults, we know it wasn't right. Yet the unconscious defenses of the fantasy bond keep us from understanding how this affects our adult relationships and we remain stuck in the pattern. I have a client whose mother used to lock her out of the house and tell her, 'You are no daughter of mine' when her behavior wasn't up to her mother's perfectionist standards. My client grew up disappointing her 'female' bosses time after time, often getting forced out of a job. However, the cause of this humiliating adult pattern was not obvious to my client!

## ABANDONMENT THROUGH ABUSE

'As a child is being abused, no one is really there for them. In the moment the abuse is occurring, they are all alone. Hence, abuse *is* abandonment'.

Children have magical, non-logical thinking and because of their egocentricity, they make *themselves* responsible for the abuse they receive from their caregivers. Small children are *totally dependent* on their caregivers for survival. They are not able to rationalize why their parents overly criticize them, neglect them or are abusive to them. They mistakenly believe, 'something's wrong with me or my parents wouldn't treat me this way'. It's never about the parents' dysfunctional or inappropriate behavior. *Children can't afford to believe anything else because it threatens their survival.* Do not underestimate the power of survival instincts and their effect on how we make meaning. This idealistic thinking, therefore, guarantees a child's survival.

## EMOTIONAL ABANDONMENT

Emotional abandonment is pervasive and there is a complete lack of awareness and understanding of exactly what it is and how it plays out in relationships - especially in our formative years. One form of emotional abandonment comes from the narcissistic deprivation of our parents. Let me explain.

In Greek mythology, Narcissus was the one who looked in the pond (mirror) and seeing his own reflection, fell in love with himself. In the early years of our lives, we need to be unconditionally loved and accepted for who we are. We also need our parents' physical presence and their behavior to reflect to us at any given moment this self-love and acceptance.

'Mirroring' needs to take place whether the child has a dirty diaper, is screaming, crying, ill, laughing or cooing, whether they're clean and quiet or dirty and noisy. This need for 'mirroring' is what Dr Alice Miller, author of *Drama of the Gifted Child*, calls our 'narcissistic supplies' and a large portion of our adult population is deprived of this. This is despite the fact that their parents may have been encouraging, sensitive and caring.

It takes a very emotionally mature adult to consistently 'mirror' back to his or her child a sense of their innate preciousness and value. Most adults are emotionally undeveloped because their emotional dependency needs were not met when they were children. These people are little children inside adults' bodies and are commonly referred to as 'adult children'. Our society is full of adult children trying to be good parents.

These emotionally immature parents *need* their children to approve of and admire them, so they can *finally* get their narcissistic needs met. This syndrome is the basis of our societies' obsession with super-achievement. Many talented, highly successful people, who have been praised and admired for their talents and achievements, suffer from this form of emotional abandonment. These achieving types will say, 'My parents were always around and took care of me, but I only ever felt loved when I was being admired and praised'. This type of person is a victim of emotional deprivation.

There is another covert form of emotional abandonment that later creates devastating consequences in adult relationships. This abandonment occurs when a parent places the child into the 'emotional surrogate spouse' role. In dysfunctional marriages, it is very common for one or both parents to bond inappropriately with one of their children. An example of this might be, if Mom is mad at Dad and is afraid to direct her anger at him; she may criticize him, complain and express her disappointments to one of the children. Or she may even ask a child for advice about Dad or the relationship.

Another example may be Mom sharing other adult problems and her feelings about them with this child because of the lack of connection and partnership in her marriage. By making the child her confidant, she is empowering him or her to feel a false sense of importance and mattering. This way of treating the child as an 'equal' (Mommy or Daddy's little man or little princess) constitutes extreme abandonment. The parents are getting their needs met at the expense of the child's needs.

Anthony was a client of mine who experienced a double-dose of emotional abandonment. Before he was born his parents migrated from a European country and could hardly speak English. Anthony was the oldest of four children and by the age of nine was handling the reading of contracts and speaking to workers at his father's business. His mother, who was left at home raising the four children, was emotionally cut off, except she would often rage. Anthony became a master at soothing his mother's rage and would often listen to her download her misery due to loneliness from her husband's constant absence. He also became an over-achiever, handling many adult responsibilities and escaped the pain of missing out on being a kid through studying.

As an adult Anthony became a high-ranking professional and married a woman who blocked intimacy by raging at him if he disappointed her. When sexual problems surfaced in the relationship, his wife made Anthony's problems 'the problem'. It was all about him and she took no responsibility for her part. She said things like, 'If people ever knew what he was really like ...'

Even though he was society's 'picture of success', when Anthony first came to see me, he told me he felt like a fraud and feared that this would be uncovered for all to see.

Again, the idea is not to blame our parents. Whatever they did or didn't do that wasn't the best was because of their own unhealed issues from their childhood. To change your relationships for the better, it's important to identify your abandonment wounds so you stop attracting partners who have your parents' worst traits and who will continue to abandon/reject you.

CHAPTER 4: BREAKING THE FANTASY BOND

## THE FANTASY BOND

Years ago I came across the groundbreaking work of Dr Robert Firestone. His primary work, *The Fantasy Bond* addresses the core reason why people fear intimacy and often don't realize it. For me his work clarified how deep abandonment wounds develop, and more importantly how, as adults, we unconsciously stop them from healing, keeping our adult problems in place. I'm referring to the wounds and deep grief we experience when we go through withdrawal from co-addictive relationships.

Simply stated, *the fantasy bond is a primary self-defense mechanism that substitutes fantasy gratification for real relating.* It is a deep unconscious process of parenting ourselves both internally in fantasy and externally forming bonds with significant others.

The fantasy bond develops in childhood as a defense against abandonment and engulfment. According to Dr. Firestone, 'the fantasy bond is a substitute for love and care that was missing in the child's world.' Many parents offer affection and love when in fact, *they feel the need for it themselves.* This type of physical affection drains the emotional resources of children rather than nourishing them. Unconsciously, the parent is stopping the child's feelings of neediness so that they don't have to feel their own feelings of neediness.

This is a form of taking, not giving and another way children are emotionally abandoned.

A former client, Lisa, came to see me because she was having trouble being close to her boyfriend. 'He isn't like your typical man,' she said. 'He's very caring and loves to hug me and touch me a lot'. The problem was that she was starting to freeze whenever he approached her and told me she thought he didn't really know her at all. She was completely baffled by this and felt guilty about her reaction to her boyfriend, whom she assured me she loved.

When we explored her childhood and any familiar feelings, she suddenly recalled how her mom would always want to touch and hug her. She felt smothered as a child and remembered her mother going up to her father at the kitchen table and throwing her arms around his neck, only for him to shrug them off. 'This happened all the time,' she told me. Realizing this, Lisa started to cry saying, 'Neither my father nor mother knew the real me. My father ignored me because he was engrossed in his work and because I wasn't a boy and my mother needed me to make her feel better and never once acknowledged that I needed my father's attention too'.

Children who are emotionally abandoned experience anxiety and a sense of emotional hunger. The more children are abandoned, the more they create an illusion of connection with a parent. This illusion is the external bond, which gives the child a sense of survival. The unconscious driving need to form the bond occurs because an emotionally abandoned or abused child has what Bradshaw calls *a rupture of their interpersonal bridge*. This rupture or wound keeps a child bonded in fantasy and as adults they transfer the bond to others, settling for a pseudo intimacy, or for other addictive behavior patterns. Although this transference initially soothes the rupture, it prevents it from healing.

## HUNGER VS. LOVE

Emotional hunger is not love. This hunger is a strong need caused by emotional deprivation in childhood. Feelings of emotional hunger are experienced as deep internal sensations that range in intensity from a dull ache to a sharp painful feeling. Because of its intensity, this sensation is often confused with real love. Many people claim to be loving and caring, when in fact they are actually feeling their emotional hunger and neediness.

Adults who are emotionally hungry become addictive, especially with relationships. They tend to mentally obsess about their partners or potential partners and are driven by their need to be loved, cherished and accepted. They are terrified of being rejected and

## CHAPTER 4: BREAKING THE FANTASY BOND

often have been. If their abandonment is triggered, they become very overwhelmed and feel out of control emotionally. If they happen to attract someone who is emotionally available and is interested in them, their fear of engulfment gets triggered and they usually sabotage the relationship because this would be an invasion of their primary defense (the fantasy bond). They (unconsciously) do things to provoke others and push them away so they can remain in the trance that has let them survive.

Debra was 38, single and not happy about it when she first came to see me. Although she had a brief marriage and several boyfriends in the past, she told me she didn't want to date any more men because she thought she was a lesbian. The thought of 'coming out' and telling her mother was upsetting her, yet she couldn't stop mentally obsessing about women.

As we explored this, Debra told me that she knew she did things to push men away and feared being close. She liked having sex with men and liked relating with men, so she was confused about the whole 'man' issue. When I inquired about her parent's relationship, she told me her father was very controlling of her mother, yet he was the one who had affairs and eventually left her.

As she was telling me about her parents' relationship, Debra suddenly remembered a thought she had before she broke up with a past boyfriend who wanted to get serious. She told me she heard the thought as her mother's voice in her head saying, 'I'm not going to let this bastard get control of me. I won't be able to get out'.

Debra also painfully recalled the phone conversation she had with her last boyfriend when he was 'dumping' her. To numb the pain of this she said to herself, 'I'll never let another man reject me again'.

Debra's obsession about being a lesbian was a defense, distracting her from feeling the abandonment pain from her relationship with her mother, who was a very self-focused woman that drank a lot when Debra was a child. Her emotional hunger from needing her mom's attention was causing Debra to obsess about attaching herself to a woman.

Coupled with her fear of being rejected by another man or having a man control her, this obsession provided a strong defense to going through her withdrawal from childhood abandonment and the accompanying separation anxiety. Doing this would break the fantasy bond and set Debra on her way to create an intimate relationship with a man - what she admitted to me she really wanted but was afraid of.

## EFFECTS ON INTIMATE RELATIONSHIPS

People have difficulty in their intimate relationships because the closeness, sexuality, and companionship threaten their internal methods of gratifying themselves. Instead of altering their defensive posture and allowing positive intrusion of friendship and love into their inner world, most people choose to distort their perceptions of their loved ones. Pulling back to a less vulnerable, more defended, place usually follows the tenderest moments in their relationships.

As an unconscious defense against intimacy, the fantasy bond is a substitute for the love and care that is missing in the child's world. This allows the child to alleviate pain and anxiety and enables them to develop a feeling of pseudo-independence. Then, as adults, they say things like,'I don't need anyone. I can take care of myself'. They try to become completely self-sufficient, needing nothing from the outer world. They withhold emotional responses from others, as well as withhold receiving from others. This is merely a more sophisticated defense against intimacy and the fear of engulfment or abandonment.

As a result of the fantasy bond, created between child and caregiver, we carry with us into adulthood the same survival mechanisms leading to a sacrifice of our freedom and any real intimacy in loving relationships in a desperate attempt to fuse with another person. Instead, we create dependencies with people, substances and behavior patterns to fill the deep emotional emptiness within us and perpetuate the illusion of the connection we so inexorably seek.

## IDEALIZED PARENT:
## THE VOICE AND THE MYSTICAL IMAGE

In order to maintain the fantasy bond, children have to idealize their parents and make themselves 'bad'. If the parents were 'bad' or sick, a child would perceive that they would not survive. Again, it's important to remember that logical reasoning doesn't factor in the set up of this emotional bondage because of the child's underdeveloped intellect.

So the fantasy bond, which makes the parents 'good' and the child 'bad', is like a mirage in the desert, giving the child the illusion that there is emotional nourishment and support in his or her life. Years later when the child leaves the parent, the fantasy bond is set up internally and is maintained by means of what Firestone calls 'the voice'.

The 'voice' represents an external point of view from criticizing, disapproving scolding or punishing caregivers (usually parents) that is now internal. A child also incorporates the attitudes that their parents held when they felt the most rejecting and angry. Sometimes the disapproval doesn't come from something that was directly said to the child, rather, something that was implied. You can also consider what was said with body language or when parents' opinions and beliefs were expressed with conviction, particularly those parents who always had to be right.

The voices in our head have been described in many different ways - inner critic; negative self-talk; stinkin' thinkin'; the committee in our head; negative beliefs; shame voice; introjected parental voices or automatic thoughts. This inner 'voice' can be experienced as quiet, doubtful, or loud. It can cause us to freeze or run on adrenaline. The voice is often partially conscious and mostly unconscious until we are in stressful situations that expose our shame or perceived inadequacies. So, you may not 'hear' the voice initially. Once you make a decision to come out of the trance and safely express your unresolved feelings, you will begin to uncover this voice that drives you to defend against intimacy. What makes the voice powerful is your lack of awareness of it.

Apart from our own childhood wounds, many of us are carrying our parents' abandonment wounds and unresolved grief from their childhoods. Bradshaw says, 'Children idealize parents through the fantasy bond and therefore they will pass the rage, hurts, loneliness and shame of their own abandonment onto their own children. Instead of passing it back where it belongs, they pass it on.'

*We unconsciously incorporate the characteristics of our parents into our personality to keep them there with us all the time, so we don't feel the pain of their abandonment of us.* This is how history repeats itself even when we've done everything in our power to *not* be like our parents.

Perhaps you can now understand why, against all rational odds, co-addicts tend to marry people who have their parents' worst traits. They are attracted to partners who will 'abandon' them. This phenomenon continues in our love relationships because we each secretly carry a 'mystical image' of an ideal partner.

This mystical image is deeply subliminal and comes from idealizing our parents. A product of our wounded inner child, we project the most powerful traits from our parents onto another person. If not our parents, we may use another 'source figure' from our childhood. We make up a fantasy partner who we believe will make up for what we didn't get in childhood, not realizing that we are recycling the past, which keeps our primary defenses in place, ensuring our survival.

Monique married the man of her dreams, Darren, a successful senior manager for a multinational I.T. Company. They had two

CHAPTER 4: BREAKING THE FANTASY BOND

children and were living an affluent lifestyle, when Darren was suddenly retrenched. Darren became bitter, blaming everyone and refused to accept less senior jobs he felt were beneath him. Eighteen months later, with Darren still unemployed, it was Monique who came to see me.

I was surprised at her unemotional, matter-of-fact demeanor. She told me that Darren had turned out to be a 'loser', just like her father, and was questioning if she ever loved Darren at all. She was starting to become attracted to other men outside the relationship, but was determined not to find another financially successful man to rescue her like her mother did.

Monique enjoyed a wealthy lifestyle in her childhood before her father became bankrupt. Her mother had left him and Monique, being the family hero, never expressed any feelings of grief about losing her father or their lifestyle.

As we worked together, Monique discovered that when she met Darren she projected an idealized image of her father, who had been a very successful entrepreneur, on to Darren. We also discovered that not only was Monique carrying her own unexpressed grief from losing her father, she was carrying her mother's unresolved grief about losing her father at 11 years old and leaving the family in debt.

*Monique's childhood abandonment pain coupled with her mother's grief was too overwhelming to cope with. This had caused Monique to shut down emotionally, confusing her about what she wanted. After she broke her fantasy bond and went through the unexpressed grief, Darren and Monique were both able to work together to become financially solvent. She also discovered new feelings of love for Darren and their connection was stronger than ever before.*

Although you may feel angry or upset from personal realizations you're getting after reading this, resenting or blaming your parents (or yourself) will keep you from healing and moving on.

It helps to remember that your parents were once hurting children with buried pain and shame. Their anger towards their parents couldn't be expressed for fear of their own survival and the anger was turned inward and became self-hatred. Your parents' defenses against their pain, shame and anger prevented them from consciously knowing it was there. If your parents were to let you express these feelings, it would have threatened their own defenses.

What you can do is grieve the losses, missed opportunities and buried feelings from the past so you stop projecting them onto others and throwing them into your future. You may also have to grieve your parents wound.

## GRIEF: THE KEY TO HEALING ABANDONMENT

You will not be able to completely heal abandonment issues from your past without allowing yourself to grieve the relationships you once may have had, but lost. It is also important to grieve the relationships you misperceived as healthy and happy.

Grief is a normal and natural response to any loss. So why do people have so much trouble fully expressing their grief? The main reason is that the great majority of people are unaware (in denial) of all the losses, especially in relationships, that they've sustained throughout their lives.

Another reason is that since expressing grief in our society is a big taboo, we are not taught how to grieve or how to deal with loss. Instead, we are constantly educated about how to acquire and hold onto things. As children, we also learn how to express ourselves by emulating the behavior of our adult caregivers. Grieving generally involves moving through intense, emotional pain and this is usually kept hidden and private. As we grew up, we learned how to suppress our grief. Because of this, most of us have massive, unresolved reserves of it inside of us. Intuitively, we fear that releasing our grief could be overwhelming and we would be 'out of control'. It is part of the human condition to fear emotionally letting go, yet this is exactly what we need to do if we are to heal our abandonment issues.

When we allow ourselves to grieve one loss, often this will trigger the release of the cumulative grief we have stored - sometimes for decades. This happened to Sally, a client of mine. Sally socialized compulsively, yet she was emotionally isolated. Her friendships were superficial and she did not have a single, intimate relationship. When one of her acquaintances, Veronica, died suddenly of an aneurism, the shock of her death pulled the plug on Sally's lifetime reservoir of stored grief. She fell apart, dramatically lost weight and had to take several weeks off work. Veronica's death had put her in touch with her stored grief and given her 'permission' to express it.

In order to heal our co-addictive relationships, we must allow ourselves to grieve over our childhood abandonment issues. Grieving will heal abandonment if we have enough time, validation and non-shaming support.

## ENOUGH TIME

The more we stop skating over our emotions and let go of trying to get a quick fix, the quicker we will go through this. Accept that it will take as long as it takes and do every thing you can to stop defending and promote healing. Imagine you want a sporting injury to heal in time for a big race. What would you do to promote the healing?

## VALIDATION

This is why you can't grieve alone. To heal emotional wounds it takes respectful witnessing from others. This is not the same as wallowing in self-pity. Most of us have shame bound to our deepest wounds. Because of the fantasy bond, we deeply feel we are bad and deserve to be punished. To expose the trauma or upset that caused the grief is something we have heavily defended. Once our defenses are safely removed and our wound is validated, we can finally heal. I have facilitated this process in healing groups for years and am still amazed when I witness the miracle of emotional healing. It does set you free!

## NON-SHAMING SUPPORT

Following on from the validation is having appropriate support. Support is not advice. In the programs we run I give instructions for three ways to support others.

1. **Sensory-based feedback:** This is simply mirroring back what you witnessed from a sensory perspective. 'I saw tears well up in your eyes.' 'I heard you raise your voice and you were talking fast.' 'I noticed your face flush.' It is especially powerful to give sensory feedback when there is incongruence in what is being said and the sensory expression. For example, when someone is debriefing something painful and they have a smile on their face; when someone is talking about something they are angry about and they are crying; when someone is talking about something very painful that happened to him or her and they are emotionally frozen with no expression.

2. **A reality check:** Reality is defined by what we think, feel, and do or not do. There are no two realities that are the same, just as there are no two people who are exactly the same. We are dealing with a double-edged sword when examining our reality. One side is that it is important for us to know what we feel, think and want to do or not do. The other side is that we may be distorted about our reality because of our history (messages received; neglect; abuse; environment; lack of instruction; etc). When you give a reality check, what you are doing is commenting on what your reality is about what was shared by another.

There is not a right or wrong evaluation put on either reality, rather just the willingness to hear someone else express his or her reality and to take that into consideration as you are sorting out your own. As in all support, both parties (the giver and receiver) gain clarity and healing from this.

3. **Sharing:** Sharing happens when one who has witnessed another's debrief has had something triggered inside them that is similar, in some way, to what has been shared. It might be an incident, a feeling, a thought or behavior. Sharing a similar experience is validating and healing for both parties. Sometimes, one feels upset by another's sharing, yet can't relate to anything similar. It is best to 'share' anyway, as the similarity may come out when sharing, as well as clarify matters for the one sharing and others in the group.

Giving feedback, reality checks and sharing your experience is a way of validating unresolved fear and pain from abandonment and engulfment in childhood. This supports the expression and release of unresolved and overwhelming emotions, which finally gives resolution. It is this resolution that contributes to lasting change and promotes clarity about what one really needs, values and wants. This is crucial for a strong personal foundation, which greatly contributes to healthy, happy relationships.

Most people in co-addictive relationships are willing to acknowledge that they have a problem and they're eager to learn skills to improve their current relationships. Skills are helpful, however, trying to apply new relationship skills without healing the abandonment and engulfment wounds of childhood is futile.

Breaking the fantasy bond and confronting the inner voice can create anxiety and start the withdrawal process. There is no deep-seated, transformational change without this accompanying anxiety.

Withdrawal from co-addictive relationships lifts us out of confusion, frustration and misery and takes us into our pain. We need our pain to heal. It enables us to be rigorously honest with ourselves and face the truth of our circumstances. The honesty and pain make an impact that helps create lasting change - away from the pain and humiliation of co-addictive relationships.

During withdrawal, we learn to let go and allow ourselves to grieve the losses we've experienced in our relationships and to close the door on past dysfunctional ones. We develop a deep intimacy with ourself, realizing what we are made of and the true inner strengths we possess. We begin to claim our dependent relationships (embracing our payoffs) instead of our dependent relationships claiming our happiness.

Once we've been through withdrawal and have broken the fantasy bond, then we are ready for intimacy and able to learn the skills and techniques necessary to build healthy relationships.

## ACCOUNTABLE ACTION

The next few exercises will help you break the fantasy bond and grieve unresolved childhood wounds regarding abandonment and engulfment. As discussed in Chapter 3, it can be helpful to have a support person, or a small group to share these exercises with, especially those who will not criticize you or try to solve your problems. If you share your responses with another, have the intent to heal, feel validated and move on. It can also be helpful to seek the support of a professional at this time, particularly someone who is trained to help people with addictive dynamics and family-of-origin issues.

There is information about programs and professionals available from my organization at *www.SetYourselfFree.com.au* You can also download worksheets for these exercises by visiting my website at *http://www.SetYourselfFree.com.au/relationships/exercises.htm.*

CHAPTER 4: BREAKING THE FANTASY BOND

## ♡ EXERCISE 12: EMBRACING ABANDONMENT AND ENGULFMENT

### Part 1

The following exercise will help you eliminate distracting, destructive and addictive behaviors that are triggered by abandonment or engulfment fears and pain you've carried from childhood experiences. As adults, we re-enact our unresolved childhood abandonment and engulfment issues even though we camouflage them in a variety of different ways. This very powerful exercise will help you to break the fantasy bond and relieve the pressure that causes you to unconsciously hold onto these dysfunctional patterns in your adult life.

You may use this exercise repeatedly to embrace abandonment or engulfment fears and pain that surface in your adult life. More importantly, the exercise will help you identify and embrace the original source of your abandonment and engulfment issues that come from childhood. To set yourself free in adult relationships it is crucial to discern if your emotional reactions are of a child feeling expression from the past or a reasonable reaction to present circumstances.

To receive optimum value from this exercise, it is important to allow your memories to connect with the feelings and the beliefs you formed from them. When you respond to the various questions in this process, make sure you note when the instructions change from using your *non-dominant hand* to your *dominant hand*. At times in the exercise I will suggest that you write with your non-dominant hand. This can help you to bypass your logical mind and connect with your feeling mind.

Find a quiet place where you won't be disturbed, and give yourself about 45 minutes. Before you begin the exercise, decide if you want to work on an abandonment or engulfment issue. Select an issue that is current or something from your recent past that you have not resolved.

*Abandonment issues* may present as fear of rejection; fear of being left or being alone; anxiety or hurt about being left out; a driving need to be needed or appreciated. You may also be caretaking, pedestalizing or overly focusing on another.

*Engulfment issues* may present as fear to commit; fear of being controlled; withdrawing; avoiding; distancing; escaping; feeling boxed in or suffocated. You may also feel better than others in some ways and feel powerful fixing another's problems.

Begin the exercise by relaxing. This will help you to connect with your feelings. Then close your eyes and allow yourself to recall in as much sensory detail as possible the situation that triggered abandonment or engulfment fear and pain.

Once you have done this *respond to the following questions using your dominant hand.*

1. My situation is:

   _____

   _____

   In order to lessen the intensity of the situation, you may now want to see what lesson you can derive from it. It is usually something that gives you value in some way and has a positive intent. *Continue with your dominant hand.*

2. What destructive, addictive or defensive behaviors did you act out in this situation?

   _____

   _____

CHAPTER 4: BREAKING THE FANTASY BOND

3. Specifically how do you feel your behavior protected you?

_____
_____
_____

4. What relationship pattern felt familiar?

_____
_____
_____

As you know, most of our unhealthy behaviors are triggers by unresolved childhood issues. In order to get to the core of this, we are going to call upon the vulnerable, childlike energy within you. It might help you to close your eyes and visualize yourself when you were a child.

Now let yourself go and travel back in time to find a situation that feels familiar to the adult situation you are examining today. Allow yourself to get in touch with your core feelings.

Once you have a recollection of a childhood situation that feels familiar to your adult situation, answer the following questions and respond in your *non-dominant hand*.

5. When did this originally occur and what happened?

_____
_____
_____

6. How did you feel about this at the time? Did you get to resolve your feelings? If not, what did you do with them? How do you feel about this now?

_____
_____

7. What limiting beliefs (about yourself and about others) did you form as a result of this incident?

_____
_____

8. What effect did this have on your life as a child? Consider your relationships or the way you related to others.

_____
_____

Take a deep breath and *change to your dominant hand.* Look upon this situation as an adult. Allow yourself to realize you may have been a victim of the situation when you were a child. Now answer these questions:

9. What effect is this unresolved abandonment or engulfment issue having on your life as an adult? Consider your relationships or the way you relate to others.

_____
_____
_____

CHAPTER 4: BREAKING THE FANTASY BOND

10. Specifically how are you different today than when this incident originally occurred? Consider your knowledge; wisdom; what you believe today; resources available to you.

_____

_____

11. What steps can you take so that you don't have to continue to react with destructive, defensive or addictive behavior?

_____

_____

Before proceeding with Part 2, it is helpful to share what you've written in Part 1 of this exercise with someone you trust, perhaps a counselor, buddy or a support group. This will help you to connect with the reality of the situation in a more realistic way.

## Part 2

As you look back upon the original incident from your adult perspective, it is easy to acknowledge that you have more wisdom, resources and experience than when the incident originally occurred. Although you have a mental understanding and know what steps you can take to conquer this, when a situation arises that triggers a core wound, you may find you feel powerless and over reactive because you are still holding the emotions you felt in childhood.

At this point in life, the abandonment or engulfment fear or pain is probably deeply embedded because you have had many re-enactments of the original incident. Therefore, every time you are faced with it, the *fear that you cannot conquer it* surfaces.

The next steps will help to change that.

*Read and then close your eyes.* Take a deep breath - relax - and call upon your past knowledge and inner wisdom. Consider the resources that are available today that you didn't have when this incident originally occurred (for examples, you may be more articulate, assertive, relaxed; also consider the strengths, talents and abilities that you have today).

*Respond to the following questions using your dominant hand.*

1. List the resources available to you today that you will use when dealing with abandonment or engulfment fear and pain (consider resources for ongoing healing; support systems; coaching/mentoring; literature; spirituality; physical movement).

   _____
   _____

2. If you are faced with abandonment/engulfment pain or fear in the future, what can you do differently to interrupt a negative behavior pattern?

   _____
   _____

3. What bottom lines are you prepared to honor so that you do not fall back into old, reactive behaviors?

   _____
   _____

## EXERCISE 13: MYSTICAL IMAGE OF YOUR IDEAL PARTNER

This is an exercise we do in my weekend programs that helps people to clearly identify how they unconsciously project an idealized image of their parents onto a current partner. This is created from the fantasy bond - 'good' parents/'bad' child. We don't realize at the time of our fantasy projection that we usually attract a partner who has our parent's combined worst and best traits. We don't see the 'bad' traits until after the infatuation wears off. This keeps us confused and is a great defense and distraction.

In essence what we do is make up a fantasy partner who we believe will give us what we didn't get from our parents. We keep trying to resolve our past with our present.

I suggest that you position this exercise as a sacred ritual. Set an intention to break the fantasy bond. The power of your intention will allow deep healing.

**Action steps**

1. Picture your mother, as she was when you were a child and adolescent. Make two lists, one of all of your mother's positive traits or characteristics and one of her negative ones.

   _____
   _____
   _____

2. Repeat the same with your father.

   _____
   _____
   _____

3. Now write down what you needed from them and never got.

   _____
   _____
   _____

4. Take a large piece of blank paper and draw a large face like the illustration on the right.

5. Combine the most positive traits of your mother and father and write them down in the left eye.

6. Combine the most negative traits of your mother and father and write them down in the right eye.

7. Now select what you needed the most from your parents and didn't get and write it across the forehead.

Take a good look at the mystical image. Set a strong intent to be complete with this pattern. Now say out loud:

- I realize you are nothing more than a childhood fantasy.
- I am now willing to let go of this illusion and break the fantasy bond.

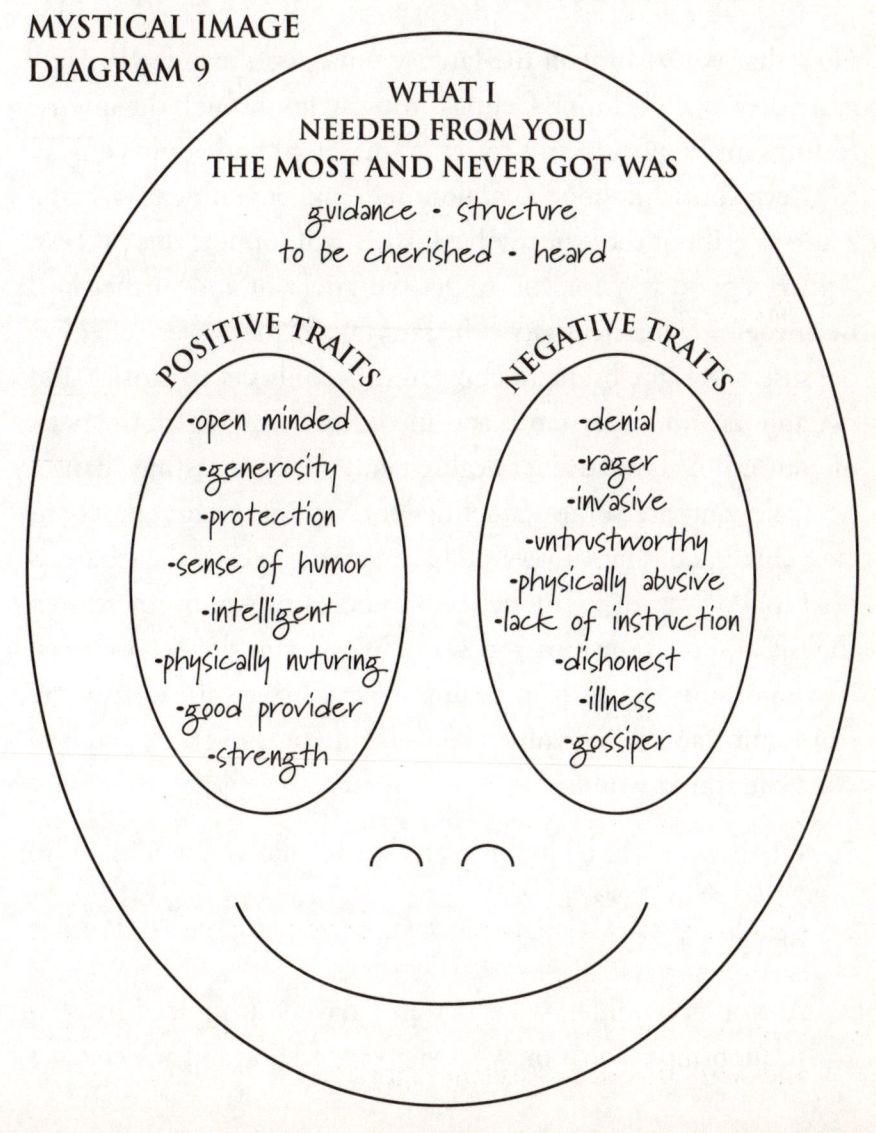

**MYSTICAL IMAGE**
**DIAGRAM 9**

WHAT I NEEDED FROM YOU THE MOST AND NEVER GOT WAS
guidance · structure
to be cherished · heard

POSITIVE TRAITS
- open minded
- generosity
- protection
- sense of humor
- intelligent
- physically nuturing
- good provider
- strength

NEGATIVE TRAITS
- denial
- rager
- invasive
- untrustworthy
- physically abusive
- lack of instruction
- dishonest
- illness
- gossiper

- TEAR UP THE PICTURE OF THE FACE.
- I acknowledge and embrace my past and now say goodbye to it.
- I choose my present knowledge and resources to support me in creating my future relationships.

## ♡ EXERCISE 14: WRITING A FAIRYTALE OF YOUR CHILDHOOD

Now that you've broken the fantasy bond, you may feel anxiety and other overwhelming feelings. You can go through the intense feelings more quickly and easily if you let go and allow yourself to grieve your childhood abandonment and engulfment. Writing a fairytale about these unresolved issues will support this process. This is a good way for you to get the grief out and further heal by engaging your creativity. The fairytale format is very effective because the right brain (feeling mind) connects to stories and metaphors and understands this medium. Engaging all the parts of your mind allows deeper healing, and therefore lasting change.

Following are some guidelines for writing a fairytale about your childhood. The purpose of this exercise is to elicit the repressed grief that drives un-useful behaviors and stops you from creating the life and relationships you want. When you finish writing it, it's important to read it to a supportive person with whom you feel comfortable being vulnerable. The intent is to grieve and heal your childhood wounds.

1. Firstly, you will be looking at your formative years (birth to 21 years) in 7-year increments, i.e. 0-7 years of age, 7-14 years of age, 14-21.

2. As you grew older, what patterns have you noticed in your relationships? Focus on what you were feeling and any changes

to your themes/stories. For your adult years, start the story with, 'and when he/she grew up' and then link your adult problems/dysfunction to your formative years.

3. It might be helpful to use a different-colored pen for each 7-year period of your life and one for your adult life - 21 years plus. Your right brain loves color.

4. Write a few paragraphs about each of these time periods. You may also use point form. Include any relationships or other changes that had a significant effect on you.

5. For each 7-year period, include as many of the following points as you can. If you can't address each point, write about the ones that stand out most in your mind, or that you feel had the biggest impact on you. Consider:

- What was your parents' relationship like? Consider physical, psychological, emotional, intellectual, spiritual, and sexual aspects, as well as affection and love.

- Your family roles, rules, beliefs, behaviors, and unmet childhood needs.

- Sayings that you remember hearing at the different periods of your life.

- Recall the characteristics of your mother and father and the methods they used in raising you.

- What was the emotional climate?

- What were the physical circumstances?

- What were the relationships like in the family, including grandparents and siblings? Consider when the siblings arrived in the family, and how this affected you.

- Were there any other significant relationships? (i.e. teachers, relatives, other people's parents, etc.)
- Were there any traumatic experiences during these times? If so, what were they, how did you feel about them and what impact did they have on the family?

# CHAPTER 5

# CREATING INTIMACY

*There's a billion people on the planet...*
*I mean, what does any one life really mean?*
*We need a witness to our lives.*
*In a marriage you're saying,*
*'Your life will not go unnoticed because I will notice it.*
*Your life will not go un-witnessed because*
*I will be your witness.'*

From the movie 'Shall We Dance'

If I were to pick one word to give a generic definition of intimacy it would be *'connection'*. This is also the general word I use to describe spirituality. Think of it, if you are spiritual, you're able to 'connect' to your authentic self; to others; to nature; to animals and to a 'Higher Power' of your own understanding (it doesn't matter what your beliefs are about a Higher Power as long as your H.P. is not you or *another* person - that would be a fantasy bond).

Many years of working with people on very personal issues have taught me this: you can't have a spiritual life without having intimacy and you can't be intimate without being spiritual. You also can't have intimacy with another unless you have it with yourself first - and you can't have that, if you haven't healed your past, especially your formative years. This is why 'Creating Intimacy' is the last chapter in this book. Like Pandora's Box, you have to go through the first four chapters to get to the HOPE.

As discussed in Chapter 1, hope is a spiritual quality. Hope relieved the suffering of Pandora and her husband. Again, the point of the story is *'evil entered into the world bringing untold misery. But Hope followed closely in its footsteps, to aid struggling humanity, and point to a happier future'. (Bulfinch's Mythology - The Age of Fable)* Going through the 'misery' of relationship dysfunction makes us stronger, casting light in the shadows of our ignorance. It's hard to explain if you haven't experienced it, but once you've gone through a deep healing, you come out the other side with hope. Hope is the place to begin a foundation for intimacy.

## INTO ME I C

Years ago one of my students told me that *Into Me I C* was how she understood the meaning of intimacy.

The first four chapters of this book helped you take an in-depth look at yourself - the 'Me'. Taking responsibility to heal your unresolved issues from the past and taking an honest look at your behavior, is the first step towards creating intimate relationships, not to mention the first step in becoming aware of how you have been teaching others how to treat you.

We also looked at different types of relationship dynamics - the 'We'. Now that you have a better idea of what it takes to create a healthy, intimate relationship, I have a question for you.

Do you still want an intimate relationship and are you willing to do what it takes to create this? If you answered yes, the next step is to focus a little bit more on 'You' and a lot more on the

'We'. If you're ready to move forward, then there are two things to pay attention to.

1.  Choosing the person you want to be intimate with and ...

    Learning to create, nurture and sustain an intimate relationship? Generally people looking for a partner put most of the attention on 'the person' (the 'You'). Who's my soul mate, the perfect person for me, someone I can put on a pedestal, idealize and who will fulfill my needs and make me feel safe, or better about myself? I think you get the picture quite clearly from the first four chapters. Although we place far more attention on the 'who' rather than the 'how', there are still some important things to consider when choosing a partner. Ask yourself the following questions and give yourself time and careful consideration when answering.

    - *Are they addictive and not willing to address this?*
      If this is true, it's like being on an exercise bike at the gym, peddling fast down a road going nowhere. This will eventually wear you out and make you old before your time.

    - *Do they have a strong personal foundation?*
      How do they balance their life? Do they meet their own needs and refuse to meet yours?

    - *Have they resolved their wounds from childhood?*
      If not, they will either unconsciously place these wounds in their personal relationships - namely, with you! Or they will use up so much energy dealing with their wounds while trying to live an adult life, that there won't be much energy left for a relationship.

    - *Do you have some shared values?*
      Having some shared values reduces conflict and attaining shared goals is extremely fulfilling.

- *Can you live with this person?*
  The attraction and fascination we have with opposites can be very frustrating when we cohabitate with them. This can be resolved if both parties are willing to negotiate some daily living conditions.

- *Do you like this person?*
  Investigate this by spending a good deal of time with this person for at least six months before you answer.

Answering the above will not only help with your selection criteria for a partner, the questions assist the process of discerning the difference between needs, values, standards and boundaries, which is essential to create intimacy. I'd like to explain the difference.

As I said before, emotional needs, as distinct from physical needs such as food, shelter, clothing, medical attention, etc. are what we *must have* to be our personal best or our authentic self. We tend to chase our needs and consciously or unconsciously set up our lives and our relationships to get them met. *Most of our emotional needs are buried so deep; we are unaware that they even exist.*

If you've ever had the experience of the same type of situation occurring over and over or the same type of people showing up in your life repeatedly, odds are there is an unmet need behind it and you are setting things up to get it met. For example, if you need approval, you'll live your life to get others' approval, almost no matter what the consequences to yourself are - and you may have surrounded yourself with disapproving people to boot! If you need to be in control you'll make sure you are in any given situation and probably complain about having too much responsibility. If you have a need to be heard, odds are you may find yourself getting very angry at those around you when that need isn't getting met - except you may not know why you are angry.

Since just about everyone has unmet needs, you really don't have to take them personally. They are just remnants from childhood, learned behavior that helped you survive the rearing process.

Boundaries and standards are a couple of ways we get our needs met and protect ourselves from other people's neediness. Boundaries are for others and standards are for you. *Standards are behaviors that you hold yourself to in order to become a better person or to be more evolved in life.* When you raise standards high enough, needs tend to fade into the background. Set standards that stretch you somewhat, but which don't cause you to fail. You can always raise them once you receive the benefit of extra energy that meeting your needs gives you.

Here are some examples of boundaries and standards from someone I know who had these needs: to get attention; to not be mistaken; to be liked and to be independent. They are specific to this person's situation and what was going on in their life at the time.

## BOUNDARIES

*I do not permit:*

people to be rude to me

people to ignore me

people to dominate me, control me or force me to do things I don't want to do

people to belittle me or make fun of me

people to yell at me or to subject me to emotional outbursts

people to interrupt me

righteous, dominant people in my life

people doing something else while I'm talking to them; I want their undivided attention.

## STANDARDS

I do not base my decisions on fear of the consequences.

I pay my bills on time.

I don't overdraw my checking account.

I return all phone calls and emails.

I speak straight, even without the 'right' words.

I ask for what I want.

I can make mistakes, particularly in front of others.

I do not need to have all the answers.

It's okay to be independent as long as the bills are paid.

I tell the truth.

I say no.

I don't spend time with people who drain my energy.

I don't suffer.

Values are a whole other kettle of fish. They are the things you naturally express or are drawn to. Values may include things like beauty, spirituality, mastery, to teach, to lead, to learn or to catalyze. The distinction here is that a need is something you've got to have; it compels you or pushes you. A value is something you naturally express; it pulls you forward, is effortless, and you may not even be aware it is a value because it is so YOU.

## CHARACTERISTICS OF INTIMACY IN A RELATIONSHIP

There are certain characteristics that nurture and sustain intimacy in relationships. I'd like to start by defining Intimacy.

I particularly like best selling author Terry Gorski's definition of an intimate relationship. He said he found it *Webster's Unabridged Dictionary.*

*Intimacy is a close personal relationship that's marked by affection, love and a depth of knowledge or broadness of information about another person.*

Let's break this down: *A close personal relationship:* Basically people need to have close proximity to each other to be intimate. How can you be intimate if you don't have close association or close personal contact? You also need 'prime time' together where your partner is a central focus in activities.

*The relationship needs to be marked by affection:* In this case affection means that I like you. You are a good friend. The friendship is unconditional, meaning that I can know your weaknesses and even horrible things about you and still care about you.

What is your relationship to the essential nature or genuine core of this person? Who are they? Can you honor who they are and do you feel good around this person (without pedestalizing)?

*Love:* I care about you for who you are and it is in my best interests for you to act in your best interests, even if I don't agree with what you feel is best for you. When we love someone, we don't have to agree with all of their standards and values, although it is important to have some in common. Having personal boundaries is very important to having loving relationships.

*Depth of knowledge:* I have got to know you; your values; your needs; what makes you tick; what you like and dislike; your strengths and your weaknesses. This requires time together and a close personal association. You can't have intimacy without having a history with someone and you can't have a history without having spent time together. It also takes talking, dialogue and communicating with each other to gain a depth of knowledge.

You can't be truly intimate with lots and lots of people. Intimate relationships are limited in numbers, maybe only three to five people at any given time, usually one or two primary relationships and a few secondary relationships. Intimate relationships have an identity of a 'We'. The two people are not enmeshed. They intermix and interweave their lives together, demonstrating an in-depth understanding and knowing detailed information about each other.

## OBSTACLES TO INTIMACY

Removing the obstacles to intimacy makes creating it a much more pleasurable *experience*. Most of this book has been about removing the barriers to intimacy. Co-addictive relationships; the addictive love dance; staying in a fantasy bond; missing bricks in people's personal foundation and throwing NEEDS into our relationships all prevent intimacy.

When relating, another confusing aspect is having the ability to discern the difference between needs, values, wants and desires and how to get them fulfilled while being in a relationship. Placing our personal needs into a relationship, expecting the relationship or our partner to meet them, not only prevents intimacy, it causes conflict. When there is a conflict with another we often pay more attention to finding out who is wrong, rather than what is wrong. *Essentially whenever we are looking for who is wrong, we are not handling our own needs.*

Our needs (even emotional ones) are linked to survival and carry some amount of fear. When our needs are not met, we feel anxious and we unconsciously place them into our relationships to get them met. When we place our needs into a relationship, we are really placing fear into the relationship.

Most of us are confused about our emotional needs and don't know how to identify them because they were unmet or neglected in childhood. At the end of this chapter there is a very powerful exercise called 'Meeting Your Needs in Relationships'. I call this exercise powerful because we use conflict resolution to help uncover your needs. The exercise helps you identify what part of a conflict is yours, which is usually the part that is driven by your need.

A romantic relationship that is initiated from sexual magnetism is another obstacle to intimacy. If sexual magnetism is more important than a bond of affection and a good friendship, then the relationship is condemned to be extremely painful and intense. The sexual draw or pull doesn't last because sexual familiarity eventually takes away the infatuation. This type of relationship is a set-up for intensity, which makes intimacy impossible and, eventually, everyone miserable.

## BOUNDARIES: THE KEY TO TEACHING OTHERS HOW TO TREAT YOU

Boundaries are basically for your protection and are the separator of you from others. Without setting significant boundaries, you can't get your needs met. Getting clear about boundaries and how to put them in place is one of the most essential things you can do to teach people how to treat you. In fact, your current boundaries - or the lack of them - are directly related to how people treat you.

Boundaries permit only the behaviors of others that are acceptable and nourishing to you. When you set a boundary, you are protecting your heart, soul and identity. You cannot be yourself without the protection provided by strong, healthy boundaries. The people who really care about you and who are worth having a relationship with will honor your boundaries. When you set new boundaries, give everyone time to get used to them. They eventually will - or they will move on. If they move on, then it's probably the best for all concerned.

Pia Mellody defines boundaries as: 'a system of limit-setting that enhances a person's ability to have a sense of self and to control the impact of reality on the self and others.' The purpose of having

## CHAPTER 5: CREATING INTIMACY

boundaries is to protect and contain your reality and to keep you from offending and violating others.

Having boundaries helps to give you a sense of your own identity. They allow you to know where you end and someone else begins. With boundaries, you can detach from others in a healthy way, without isolating. Only when you can do that, can you begin to have intimacy with yourself, which is the key to having intimacy with others.

Boundaries keep you from being enmeshed and fused in your relationships. When you're *fused*, you usually become *confused*, which makes matters appear difficult and overwhelming. Then, it's almost impossible to define and separate yourself from another in a healthy way. You'll begin to feel engulfed, as if you don't have your own privacy, causing you to put up walls and isolate from others as a seeming solution.

Sometimes we use walls of fear, anger, talking, smiling, busy-ness, and so on to shut people out and to protect ourselves. Operating behind these walls prevents intimacy and, after a while, we can become very lonely. Loneliness triggers deep abandonment pain and feelings of inadequacy. Being lonely for too long can drive us to 'trust' (or should I say try) again, and get involved in another relationship. But because most of us haven't learned how to set boundaries, we collapse our walls to 'get close' and become too open with no protection. By doing this we are teaching others how to treat us and we set ourselves up to get hurt.

Remember, co-addicts swing in polarities from one extreme to the other. On one side of the pendulum they're too open with no protection, setting themselves up to be hurt. On the other side they're walled off from others, feeling isolated and lonely. These lines from a poem by Kent Dixon called *'These Walls'* illustrate the pain of isolation we feel when we have walls rather than boundaries.

*These walls are tall to break my fall*

*These walls are inside so I can hide*

*These walls are real so I won't feel*

*They rise high above so I won't love*

*These walls are near so I won't fear*

*These walls impair so I won't care*

*These walls are high so I won't cry*

*These walls won't leave so I might believe*

*That in the space beyond the stone I'm not alone'*

Boundaries are not rigid like walls. Rather, they are flexible, acting as a block and filter to offences, intrusions and abuse. They help you to define, contain and separate your reality from another's. These realities are:

*Physical:* how you observe and behave in your environment;

*Intellectual:* how you assign meaning to the things you observe and do in your environment;

*Emotional:* the connection you have with yourself, others, the earth, animals and a power greater than you.

Reality is a matter of perception and each of us is responsible for our own reality. There is not another person on this earth whose reality is the same as yours, because no one has walked in your shoes. If there are cracks in your personal foundation, you have unconsciously learned to take on other people's thoughts, feelings and behavior patterns and thereby not had much freedom of conscious choice. Setting boundaries helps you to attain freedom because boundaries act as a container for your reality. Without them, you will be a victim or a persecutor of others - or both!

In building boundaries, you are working on your identity and if you've been raised in a functional family, you've been dealing with this from puberty onwards. The more that you are able to build and maintain healthy boundaries, the more you will be able to let go of control in your relationships. People in co-addicted relationships have impaired boundaries, which leads to elements of control and manipulation. However, it wouldn't be appropriate to let go of control without some sort of protection. The degree to which you can protect yourself in a functional way with boundaries is the degree to which you can finally relax, let go and begin to trust (yourself and others) because you feel that your boundary system is intact. Boundaries are imperative in learning how to let go and trust, particularly in our intimate relationships.

## TYPES OF BOUNDARIES

There are basically three types of boundary systems: internal, external and spiritual. Within these, there are four components:

The external components are physical and sexual; they function outside of the body and control distance and touch with others. Physical touching is about nurturing whereas sexual touching is about arousal or lust. People in addictive relationships often confuse the two.

For those with weak personal foundations, the internal boundaries are the most damaged. The internal components are emotional and intellectual. Internal boundaries act like a filter, letting things in and out. I often suggest to clients to imagine they are like window screens - they let the fresh air in and keep the bugs out. Protecting your thinking and feeling realities, internal boundaries allow you to jettison things that are not true for you. For example, if someone accuses you of hurting them, with a healthy internal boundary you would be able to take that information in, think about it, have some feelings about it and easily decide if it were true or not - without being defensive. Perhaps you didn't offend that person and they're 'hurt' because their attempted manipulation of you failed. (e.g. your mother complains that you're hurting her feelings because you can't visit her this weekend). An internal boundary will facilitate you to allow others to have their own reality, even when it conflicts with yours. This occurs in two forms:

1. Say that someone gives an appraisal of you that you feel is not true. You don't have to defend yourself or argue with them. You can simply allow them their opinion of you without it affecting your own opinion of yourself - as long as it's not a statement of offence (such as 'you're stupid' vs. 'I don't think you have the capabilities for this job').

2. Say you and a co-worker have differing opinions about your organization ('the company is great and provides opportunities for advancement' vs 'the company is lousy and doesn't offer us a chance to get ahead'). With healthy internal boundaries, you can agree to disagree.

If another's reality conflicts with yours and you wish to stand firm in yours, you can do this by closing your mouth and saying it silently to yourself. Doing this helps you take ownership of your own reality and value yourself. You cannot do this if you lack good, internal boundaries because without them, you can't get enough separation from another to resist owning their reality - even when it doesn't sit well with you. Exceptions to this are counselors, coaches, mentors and other people who you have invited to comment and assist you in clarifying your reality. A spiritual boundary occurs when two people are being intimate with one another while both of them are using their external and internal boundaries. This allows them to expand and experience spirituality, the essence of their wholeness, together.

## GUIDELINES FOR COUPLES REMAINING IN A RELATIONSHIP

It is possible to recover from a co-addicted relationship without ending the relationship. Although a great challenge, it also provides a tremendous opportunity for personal growth and intimacy building. However, both parties must be willing to follow some guidelines in order for them to work effectively.

It is best to make a mutual co-existence pact, which works like a contract. There is usually a time limit of one year on the pact in which each of the parties agrees not to end the relationship. For example, you may agree to continue living together and have 'time out' occasionally. 'Time out' (a few days to a week apart) can be called by either person for the purpose of self-care and well-being. You may agree not to have sex for a designated period of time (especially if one or both partners are sex addicts). If you're living together, you may have a special room which you declare 'off limits' to the other person. You can make any types of agreements that you want, as long as you both agree and as long as your contract incorporates at least the following specific guidelines:

1. Don't assign blame when you're in a conflict.

2. Do not keep score on your partner.

3. Do not threaten abandonment when you're in conflict.

4. Do not argue or debate about facts or perceptions, so you can be right.

5. Do not lecture, counsel or instruct your partner unless you were asked for your advice or suggestions.

6. If you have an upset, you can usually communicate it in four sentences, which are statements, not questions. It is important to stay with your own awareness, using 'I' statements. First, say to yourself: 'What is it that I ...

- see and hear
- interpret
- feel
- want

For example, 'I heard you slam the door. I gather from this that you're angry about something or maybe you're angry with me. I feel frightened of your anger and I'm afraid you might leave me. I would like you to tell me what's going on.'

When we communicate in this manner, we may be surprised to find that, metaphorically speaking, it was only the wind that slammed the door.

Once you've set up this type of contract and begun following these guidelines, there will be a lot less talking and emptiness in your relationship. This stage of recovery often features a great amount of fear and panic because the addictive part (the pseudo-intimacy, which is really a false connection established through fighting and intensity) has stopped. This is when you'll confront whether you do have enough between you to continue the relationship. This is also the time to re-approach your partner about what your needs, wants and desires are. After some time has passed, write an inventory of what healthy needs, wants and desires are being met in your relationship.

The key to building a healthy, intimate relationship with your current partner (even if it's been addictive) lies in the willingness of you *both* to take the necessary steps to participate in your recovery.

I believe the most effective way to heal relationships for couples who are co-addictive is to set up a mutual co-existence pact as outlined above, and then initially to detach emotionally. This is a bigger challenge than it appears to be because these couples are used to being enmeshed and focusing on the other. Then I ask them to focus on themselves (not their relationship or their partner) and work on their unresolved family-of-origin issues, strengthening their personal foundation and to treat any prevailing addictions.

CHAPTER 5: CREATING INTIMACY

If addictions are present, I suggest that in tandem with their personal healing work, they separately attend relevant twelve-step meetings such as Alcoholics Anonymous or Al-anon. After focusing on foundational issues and experiencing healing (this is individual and could range from six months to two years), they are then ready for couple counseling and to learn strategies and skills for healthy relating. For most couples, especially those with addictive personalities or those with unresolved issues from childhood, marriage counseling does not work!

## THE FIVE STAGES OF PARTNERSHIP

Couples go through stages in their relationships. The process of creating intimacy with another is evolutionary and transformative, which involves change. People are frightened when transformational changes occur - especially in their close relationships. It brings up the fear of loss. For that reason, I feel it's important to recognize the changes these stages bring and to understand how and why they are necessary to creating intimacy.

There is much information available on stages people go through in their relationships. The best I've found that makes the most sense and is easy to apply comes from my friends and colleagues, Layne and Paul Cutright. Layne and Paul are bestselling authors and masters in helping people create powerful partnerships. I am delighted to have their permission to include the five stages of partnership from their e-course 'How to Create Powerful Partnerships'. You can down load this exercise from *www.shirleysmith.com/fivestages.html*

Understanding the five stages of partnership is like having a map for your relationship. It will help you to understand where you are now, where you've been and what stages lay ahead in the future as you grow in your partnership. Many have said that just learning about the five stages of partnership has explained so much of what was troubling them about their relationships.

## 1. ATTRACTION

This stage of relationships is characterized by a fascination with another person, organization or project and a desire to learn more about them, as well as a desire to share about yourself with the other person. It's fun and it feels good. This is the time when positive possibilities are sensed and explored. This is the stage people wish would last forever.

## 2. POWER STRUGGLE

This is the stage where people start testing each other. It is one of the most difficult stages for people. Who is going to get whose way and how? Distrust from your unresolved past manifests and there is often a fear of loss of control and heavy judgments of the other person start to show up. Many relationships never move beyond this stage and many end here. This stage is really about building trust.

## 3. CO-OPERATION

This is the stage where you learn to trust one another and to resolve upsets to your mutual satisfaction and benefit. You learn to share power and appreciate each other's unique abilities and gifts. However, it is still self oriented: 'What can I get out of this relationship?' rather than 'What can we create *with* this relationship?'. Beware of false co-operation in which one person acquiesces to the other in order to 'keep the peace'. This is still power struggle, only in a more subtle form.

## 4. SYNERGY

This is the stage where there is a realization of a power greater than that of each individual. There is also a commitment to a specified focus and use of the power. Extraordinary satisfaction, intimacy, and a deep sense of mutual trust, empowerment and ease characterize this stage. It is a highly creative, high-performance relationship. It also possesses a high level of acknowledgment and appreciation. The relationship emanates joy and power in this stage.

## 5. COMPLETION

This is a stage many people fear and avoid dealing with altogether. There are four ways relationships can be completed: drifting apart, expulsion/ejection, conscious completion or death. Sometimes completion is only about changing the form of the relationship, not necessarily the end of the relationship altogether. Generally, the problematic stages for most people are power struggle and completion. Because of this, I have added more information from Layne and Paul's course on these two very challenging stages.

**Power struggle**

People often ask us if the power-struggle stage is necessary. Who wouldn't want to avoid power struggle? People don't exactly jump up and down with excitement when they enter that stage, like they might in the attraction stage! *What most people don't understand is that the power-struggle stage is really an opportunity to build trust at a deeper level.* And trust is necessary if a relationship is to mature. Power struggle isn't bad; it's just inevitable, predictable, unavoidable and recurrent. That is, it happens more than once in any long-term relationship. Why? Because each time you increase the commitment in a relationship, e.g., investing more time, money, emotion, etc., more trust is required. *Whenever more trust is required, you will temporarily revisit power struggle.*

**Completion**

The other problematic stage is completion. Everything that is created has a beginning, middle and end. And that includes your partnerships.

There are four ways partnerships end:

1. DEATH

   The first is obvious, as when one of the partners dies.

2. DRIFTING APART

   The second is when geography, time, interests or a slow build-up of withheld communications may separate partners.

3. ABRUPT EXPULSION

   The third occurs with an apparently irreconcilable upset and the partnership is abruptly ended, usually with very bad feelings.

4. CONSCIOUSLY WITH LOVING INTENT

   Obviously, the most desirable of the four is consciously with loving intent, but most people don't know how to do that.

Conscious completion includes acknowledging what you have learned from the partnership, what you have contributed to the partnership, making any apologies that might be necessary and asking for and extending forgiveness.

*Often, completion is about changing the form of the partnership, not ending the relationship altogether,* as in parents who are divorcing or former business partners who are members of the same professional association. Their relationship will no longer be in the form of marriage, but they will continue to be partners at some level in co-parenting their children. In this case, conscious completion is very important for developing or maintaining mutual respect, dignity and caring in the partnership.

Your capacity to complete partnerships harmoniously for the good of all concerned is a reflection of your spiritual maturity. It is a worthwhile goal.

## SEVEN STEPS TO BUILDING HEALTHY RELATIONSHIPS

Healthy relationships aren't 'made in heaven'. They take work, time and are built progressively, a step at a time. To those in pursuit of the quick fix, this may sound like a drag, but actually there is a lot of adventure, fun, laughter and personal insights to be enjoyed along the way.

Below are seven steps to building a healthy relationship:

1. Picture the relationship that you want. Visualize this relationship as a separate entity, a common path and ask yourself what you are willing to give to it. Then ask yourself, 'What will I allow and what will I not allow within this relationship?'. It is important to be focused on this, so write it down. You may also desire to write out an ideal scene for this relationship, incorporating in it your needs, wants and desires, as well as what you will give to the common path. Many times we experience an undesirable situation in our relationships, not because we wanted it, but because we didn't take the time to specify what we *didn't* want. Clarity in this latter situation is as imperative as clarity in the former.

2. Consider the steps you'll take to begin the formation of the relationship (eg. be more social, take more risks when you fear rejection, take a course which helps you express yourself better).

   Ask yourself what type of person you desire to join with and in which manner (lover, friend, etc). A word of caution: this step is to come from your desires, not from your fears. If you choose to join with someone out of fear, what you may do is allow yourself to join with someone for fear of not having anyone. If you already have a partner in your life, you may join together to decide the steps that you'll take on your common path.

3. This step is about issues of control and co-operation of both yourself and others. Look at how you control others emotionally and how you allow yourself to be controlled emotionally. It is important for each of us to learn how to control ourselves positively and to remain in control of our own reality. We need to learn how to co-operate with others without giving ourselves away. Often, we give our power away by not controlling ourselves and we unconsciously send out a message that we need to be controlled. If this is going on in your relationship, this is unbalanced co-operation. You must decide and discuss with your partner where you both are willing to co-operate and where you are not.

4. Define how you want to join with them in terms of how close or how separate you wish to be. Determine what is appropriate for you at this time. This step involves practicing being separate (containing your own reality) while you share a common path with another - without taking on their fears, anger, pain, judgments, etc. Boundaries will help you with this step.

5. Ask yourself how you can best place your talents, abilities and actions to cause this to happen. Look at how you can harmonize your needs, wants and desires within the relationship. Work out your own balanced recipe.

6. Examine your past and draw from your knowledge to give you insights so that you won't repeat the same dysfunctional patterns. All mistakes are opportunities for the beginning of new creations, so draw strength and wisdom from your past mistakes. However, as you reflect on the past, do not dwell upon it. Rather, accept it, embrace it and use it as a tool to help you in your life today. Your fears are held in the past. In order to create a healthy, balanced relationship, you may at

this time want to release any fears that are standing in the way of achieving this. I recommend using the process called Embracing Fear, which is in my first book *Set Yourself Free - a must read for people caught in addictive behaviors and those who love them.* You can order or read more about it at my website *http://www.SetYourselfFree.com.au*

7. This last step encompasses looking at the past, present and future. When you look at your relationships from this overall perspective, you are looking into all possibilities. Perhaps there are things that you have not experienced in your relationships yet, but you'd like to. Opening yourself up through assuming this overview on your life may stir your imagination and bring about new desires. However, it may also bring forward more of your fears. In order to have truly satisfying relationships and fulfill your hearts' desires, you must be willing to release your fears and know in the core of your being that you deserve these relationships. If you feel blocked with this step, perhaps you need to go within and discover the core fear behind realizing and having what you really want. Perhaps, deep down you feel unworthy of having a balanced, loving, giving, healthy relationship. Perhaps if you did achieve such a relationship, your life would be devoid of drama and high intensity. How would you know if you were *really alive* then?

If you take these seven steps in the order they are given and build your relationships in that way, they will be balanced, healthy relationships. When you come together too fast with another, it creates chaos. When you come together slowly, a step at a time, it will create the balance and intimacy that you desire.

To develop intimacy with another requires years of shared time. Intimacy grows from two people building a history together. You can't have intimacy without a shared history. Intimacy with another is impossible if you don't first have intimacy with yourself.

In an intimate relationship, each person is able to share an internal experience with the other, who can listen, receive and acknowledge the communication.

Our addictive relationships have been built using the above steps - in the reverse order, starting with step seven and ending with step one. For the love addict, the scenario goes something like this:

7. You sit down and write out your laundry list for your ideal mate, allowing your imagination to run riot with your desires and referring to your past to remember to exclude what you *don't* want. You open yourself to all possibilities - now! And then, whammo! You meet him or her.

6. Once you've met him or her, you're on red alert to ensure that this is the right relationship. Because your coming together was so explosive, the honeymoon period is over quickly and in the fall-out, familiar fears from the past begin to emerge.

5. You feel out of balance and chaotic at this point and thus you haven't got a clue about what talents and abilities of your own to apply in the relationship. So you begin to focus on your partner to discover their recipe for balance, hoping it will rub off on you.

4. At this point, because the relationship was forged so quickly and is now doing so much for you, you begin to lose your own identity and you become enmeshed. You lose sight of where you and they begin and end.

3. By now, you're in so deep, you start controlling everything and everyone, including yourself because you're afraid you won't get what you want. You have no idea of how to negotiate and co-operate and sometimes you allow yourself to be controlled because you feel inadequate.

CHAPTER 5: CREATING INTIMACY

2. You realize that the person you're with isn't anything like the one on your original laundry list and you can see that you joined with them out of fear rather than desire. You decide to take some steps! You look for a self-help book or a course to take. You may go into therapy or drag your partner into couple counseling. Or perhaps, you're just looking for a quick fix and you consider dumping them in favor of someone 'better'.

1. You're really addicted at this point, so your fear of abandonment will be great, so great, in fact, that it obscures your clarity about what you will allow and what you will not allow in your relationship. You probably don't even have a clue about what you want, how to get your needs met or what your desires are.

Sound familiar? I've included this information for the purpose of self-observation, not self-indictment. All I'm really saying here is: don't beat yourself up. Instead, the next time you do the 'love dance', make sure you learn your steps in the right order!

As you can see, there is a lot involved in creating intimacy. It is a journey, a spiritual one where you have the privilege of witnessing another's life and where your life will not go un-witnessed. Intimacy gives your life meaning; lets you experience a sense of belonging; provides an opportunity for human mastery; and is an exciting adventure allowing you to make a significant impact on another's life. Does it get much better than this?

## ACTIVE ACCOUNTABILITY

The following exercises are designed to help you create intimacy. The exercises can be used repeatedly as your issues surface or when addressing different relationships. To assist you with this, you can download worksheets from my website at *http://www.SetYourselfFree.com.au/relationships/exercises.htm*

Most of our emotional needs are buried so deep; we are unaware that they even exist. One of the main causes of conflict and barriers to intimacy is when we unconsciously expect our unmet needs to be met by our partner or by the relationship. This is what drives over-reactive behavior and recycles the same frustrating and painful patterns.

Believe it or not, conflict has a benefit. It provides the opportunity to uncover your unmet needs so you can take responsibility to get them met. Meeting your own needs makes you more attractive to others; increases your confidence and self-esteem; restores your freedom of choice; enables more self-control; and provides the foundation for creating intimacy. When most of my clients try to identify their unmet needs they either draw a blank or go into confusion.

Recently, one of my clients sat down to do an exercise on identifying and meeting his needs. He couldn't do it and told me he felt like a ferret was running around inside of him. He was anxious, confused and kept distracting himself by running to the fridge. Later, when a conflict with his wife came up, he was able to identify his need (which was an unmet one from childhood) and he set some strategies in place to meet his need as an adult. Conflict is useful if you are prepared to take responsibility for your own growth.

Once you identify the unmet need it is easy to separate the childhood, emotionally reactive, expression, from the adult expression. The adult part of you can figure out how to get this met once the childhood emotion is removed.

For example, Anna and Matt used to fight when Matt was late picking her up (which he was frequently). Anna was convinced that Matt simply didn't care and this would justify her angry behavior. When she did the following exercise, Anna discovered the emotional trigger was her need to be remembered, especially to be important enough to be remembered.

When Anna was a child her father often forgot to pick her up or forgot other promises he made to her. Each time Matt forgot to be on time, Anna had a childhood, emotional reaction of fear and pain, which she learned to quickly bury and cover with anger. Once she realized she was reacting from a childhood wound, Anna was able to meet her need to get home by making alternative arrangements rather than relying solely on Matt. Anna stopped blaming Matt and took responsibility to meet her own needs. Once she had separated her unmet childhood need (to be remembered by her father) with her adult need (to get home) she was able to deal with Matt's lateness without overreacting. Anna could later share with Matt, without accusation or blame, how she felt about him running late. Matt heard and acknowledged Anna for her feelings about his tardiness; he is now seldom late and Anna can also see he remembers her in many other ways.

The purpose of this exercise is for you to evolve personally, create more intimacy and uncover your unmet needs through conflict resolution. As I said before, when there is a conflict, disagreement or upset with another, often we pay more attention to finding out who is wrong, rather than what is wrong. *Essentially, whenever we are looking for who is wrong, we are not handling our own needs.* The quickest and most efficient way to resolve a conflict with another is to confront the issue internally within our self first.

In the exercise below there are seven questions. Because you are dealing with buried needs and emotions, some of the answers may not make sense. Let yourself engage in the process and keep answering the questions because sometimes you'll get clear only after you've finished the exercise.

I've given examples from each partner in a conflict. I've done this to give you insight about how patterns often dovetail, making the conflict seem bigger and more potent than it actually is. When you do the exercise, you will only be looking at yourself and giving answers for your part.

### ♡ EXERCISE 15: MEETING YOUR NEEDS IN RELATIONSHIPS

Select an issue where you and another are in an emotionally charged conflict. Find a private and comfortable place where you won't be disturbed. Write the issue in the space below. I have put examples in italics to illustrate the process and given answers from each partner's perspective. When you do the exercise, only write your answers. If you and a partner are both doing this exercise, do it separately. You can compare notes later if you like, although this is not necessary.

You can download a blank copy of this exercise from our website at *http://www.SetYourselfFree.com.au/relationships/exercises.htm* or you can write your answers on a blank piece of paper.

The following is an example of a conflict between a married couple.

**The conflict:**

MARY

*I am upset because my husband pressures me about having sex. I don't feel aroused because I feel that he wants something from me! If I don't give in, then I either feel guilty or that I will be punished in some way (silent treatment or angry accusations).*

JOHN

*I am upset because my wife and I hardly ever have sex because she says no. I feel that she is the one that gets to call all of the shots!*

Ask yourself the following questions regarding the relationship issue/conflict you are working with:

**Why is this issue important to me (only to me and not just my partner)?**

Keep the focus on yourself and simply explore why this issue is important to you. In other words, don't make the issue bigger or more intense attempting to figure out why your feelings about the issue should be so important to your partner. Answering this question is going to define your own state of need with regard to the issue.

1. **What is your need within the issue?**

    Go back and review the information on needs in Chapter 1 and revisit Exercise 2: Assessing Your Unmet Needs.

    Once you define your need, allow yourself to own it - accept it and then have the willingness to work with it.

## MARY

*When John initiates having sex, I often feel that I don't have a choice. Once we start making love, then I have to go through with it whether I want to or not. Sometimes, once we get going, I discover that I am not in the mood. My need is to have the freedom to say yes or no.*

## JOHN

*Making love helps me to maintain a connection and intimacy with my wife. My need is to feel and maintain my masculine energy, which, to me, also equates to strength, autonomy and being supportive.*

2. **What steps can I take to meet my needs within the situation rather then holding the other person responsible for them?**

When two people each have a stake in something, it's important to understand that each individual cannot have the situation exactly the way they want it. Until you discern what your need is within the issue, ALL the conflict looks like it is about your unmet need.

Realize this and accept your need is probably different than the need of the other person involved in the conflict. Even if you should both have the same need, it is still your responsibility to meet yours and not your responsibility to meet theirs. This realization makes getting your need met within your control.

Once you identify what part of this issue is your need, then you must be willing to take some steps to meet your needs. You can only deal with a common issue once you have defined your need.

## MARY

I will let John know that the block in our lovemaking is about my need to have the freedom to say yes or no, not about him or that I don't desire him as a man. I will ask John to experiment with me in our lovemaking. If we start making love and I am not able to be aroused, (for whatever reason) can we then look for an alternative that satisfies both of us? Perhaps John can masturbate in front of me while I watch and encourage him to take pleasure.

I will find ways to relax my mind to prepare myself for lovemaking.

I intend to take the pressure off myself to become aroused and just be present with each experience, letting the energy flow.

## JOHN

I will find ways to meet my need for sexual release and connection to masculine energy, perhaps through masturbation while Mary encourages me to do so.

CHAPTER 5: CREATING INTIMACY

I will identify how I contribute to the relationship with regards to money security, support and strength. I realize that taking care of our physical environment is an important way I provide support and strength. If I feel Mary is taking this for granted, I will speak up and let her know.

If both of the above are in place, I will feel a sense of autonomy within myself, which prevents me from feeling lost in the relationship.

Step three has two parts.

**Part 1: Determine what you are really co-operating with in this situation.**

This step will help to release you from power struggle. To do this, you have to take a very honest look at yourself. See who or what it is that you are actually co-operating with. Are you fooling yourselves by thinking you are having a discussion (perhaps a heated one) with different opinions? Many times we are focusing on, and co-operating with getting OUR idea across rather than resolving the issue for the good of the relationship. If that's what you are doing, THEN DO IT INTENTIONALLY and own the fact that you are simply trying to convince the other person to support your idea.

## MARY

Many times I have used excuses about why I don't feel like having sex. These excuses are usually logical, and therefore let me get my way. I have been co-operating with me getting my way.

## JOHN

I have felt somewhat victimized by Mary and have realized that I am comfortable staying in the victim role. This role keeps me from taking responsibility for looking at what I am doing or not doing in order to feel respected or be heard.

Doing it intentionally lets you realize that your idea has validity whether the other person supports it or not. Your idea has value, whether the other person thinks so or not.

**Part 2: State the real need that you would like co-operation with.**

### MARY

I need to have the right and the freedom to choose. I want to have my choices not necessarily agreed with, but accepted by John.

### JOHN

I realize that I want satisfying lovemaking as an outer expression of my inner need to be heard and respected in my relationship with Mary.

4. **Regarding my need, what is mine, what is not? What are the wants connected to this need that is appropriate for this issue and for the relationship? The clarity from the last step gives you the capacity to determine the difference between your need, and the useful, relevant wants of the relationship.**

### MARY

I now realize that John is not pressuring me for sex. I simply have a need to have the freedom to say yes or no. I can take steps to meet my need. I don't have to feel like I am going to be punished or rejected if I don't do what an important man (read father) wants.

I want pleasurable, connected sex/love making that continues to evolve.

### JOHN

I can't expect Mary alone to meet my need to feel my masculinity. I need to be proactive outside the relationship to meet my needs to feel strong, supportive and autonomous. Rather than feeling lost

CHAPTER 5: CREATING INTIMACY

and bullied like I did in my childhood, I will take responsibility to meet my needs to be heard and respected.

I want a more connected, intimate relationship with Mary. I want our lovemaking to be more frequent and satisfying for me.

5. **Why is it so important that the other person fulfils my need? What is missing from me that when I fulfill the need, it will bring more harmony and balance, not only to me, but the situation/relationship?**

Once you have better discernment you have the capacity to start creating harmony. Answer the above questions with the intention of bringing harmony and balance to the situation.

## MARY

If I do what a man wants me to do, in the way he wants me to do it, I won't enjoy it. If I get to choose what I want to do, then I have a greater chance of enjoying it. This is why I have wanted John to meet my need for freedom by accepting my decision to say yes or no without retribution. What's missing from me is the willingness to let John have his feelings about my decision and in turn to accept him for what he wants, to accept that his choice is not meant to hurt or deprive me.

## JOHN

I have mistakenly looked to my wife to fulfill my need to be heard and respected in order to make me feel like a credible man. What's missing from me is a core belief that I am enough within the relationship just as I am.

Being in a state of balance gives you the capacity to scan your life for similar instances. At this point, you may see that this situation is a familiar one, a pattern you've played out in many of your relationships so far. Looking at it honestly may reveal that rather than being co-operative, you are actually being controlling.

6. **Look at your past and recall the times and relationships where similar issues have occurred.**

List these instances.

## MARY

My first husband wouldn't let me work outside of the home. I felt like a prisoner with no choice.

My father never allowed me to date boys or even go out in cars with my girlfriends.

Asking my father for something I really wanted usually got a 'no'.

My eldest child has always been demanding, wanting something from me. If I didn't give it, she would punish me by withholding her love and not speaking to me.

## JOHN

As a teenager having interactions with my father, it was his way or the highway.

I gave my first business partner my power because I felt he was older and wiser.

In another business partnership with my older brother, who was the family hero, my ideas weren't perceived as credible.

I entered into a highly sexual and co-addicted relationship as rescuer. I started out feeling powerful, masculine, heard and respected. I deteriorated into a debt-ridden situation, which rendered me powerless to control any of my surroundings.

Once you get to the place where you can see the patterns repeating, you will see more and more of the truth and get a truer glimpse of your interaction in the situations. *Examine this more carefully. You might discover patterns where:*

- You become insistent on others.
- You struggle with your own sense of how to do things.
- Other people appear to disagree with you or you have different opinions.

In other words, you begin to see you and the character traits you possess. This is when you can finally see what you have been teaching everyone else about you and how you have unconsciously been teaching them to treat you. This valuable information can change your life! More importantly, it can be your greatest catalyst as a motivation for change. This is how taking responsibility can set you free, rather than bog you down.

At this point, you can allow yourself choice. Once you have true choice, you then have the ability to interact from a sense of wholeness rather than neediness.

**7. Coming from a sense of wholeness within yourself, what do you now choose?**

Let yourself find the answers that aren't too fixed. Look for answers that allow you to interact. Doing this lets you confront the issue rather than the person.

## MARY

*I will ask John if we can create special times where we can 'play' at lovemaking, without expecting a certain result. During this time, I will pay attention to my internal experience and see what it is that makes me feel like I am not safe.*

*If I don't feel safe, I will work out a way, with John, to create safety and respect for both of us.*

*I know I have a strong history of reacting to my father's extreme* control of me. Rather than projecting my Dad onto John, if I feel controlled I will stop and confront myself first.

I will look at managing my energy and minimizing stress so I can respond rather than react.

### JOHN

I choose my own path without getting permission or acknowledgment from others. I don't have to be someone different than I am already. I will say what I want without defending it.

I will put attention on what and how I am communicating to Mary and if necessary, I will learn some new communication skills.

I won't project my authority figure issues on to Mary. If I find myself feeling 'not enough', I will ask her if she thinks I am inadequate in the situation.

The next time I catch myself being judgmental with Mary, I will stop and ask more questions instead of seeing and making judgments.

The next time you have a conflict in a relationship, stop the conflict with the person and start confronting the issue. Look for your unmet need within the issue. Stop yourself and recognize the other person doesn't need to know anything about what you have to say. Instead ask yourself: *What is there about this issue that concerns both our relationship and us? What is it that I would like to say to myself about this?* This is the part that belongs to you, not the other person, so answer it for yourself, rather than to prove anything to another.

If you are not feeling resolved or complete with this exercise, then you need to go deeper and be willing to be more honest with yourself. You can wait 24 hours or proceed to Question 1 now and repeat all seven questions of the exercise. Run through the seven questions (in order), as many times as you need to, until you feel there is resolution.

## EXERCISE 16: HOW TO SET BOUNDARIES

Following are some guidelines for how you can set different boundaries. As a general rule, when setting boundaries, ask yourself the following questions:

- What am I not allowing that I want to be allowing?
- What am I allowing that I shouldn't be allowing?
- How do I feel about this?
- How am I putting up walls and isolating myself?
- How do I feel about this?

**Physical boundaries**

The first thing to do is to visualize you being protected (perhaps in a white light, or a large glass jar like a bell, or being enveloped by a series of gold rings from head to toe). This physical boundary is flexible and moves according to whom you're with - it may contract when you hug someone and expand to provide extra protection when you're in a crowd.

In setting this boundary, there is one statement to memorize: 'I have the right to determine when, where, how and with whom I want to be touched, and how close I'll allow you to stand next to me. And you have the right to do the same with me.'

**Sexual boundaries**

The sexual boundary is similar to the physical boundary, but it is important to note that even when you're being sexual with someone, you still maintain a boundary ... on your skin.

The statement to memorize here is: *'I have the right to determine with whom, where, when and how I'm going to be sexual. And you have the right to do the same with me.'* This means that if you want to negotiate being sexual with someone and they decline, that's the end of it. A sexual boundary allows you to be sexually appropriate and protective of yourself.

### Emotional and intellectual boundaries

You cannot set these internal boundaries until you have set your external ones. When you visualize the internal boundaries, picture something that acts like a filter. Perhaps a window screen?

The statement to memorize here is: *'I create what I think and feel and I am in control of what I do or don't do. The same is true for you.'*

You can also add: *'My reality is derived more from my history than from what you are saying or doing in front of me. And the same is true for you.'*

The caveat to this is that although you are not responsible for another's responses, you must note the impact of your behavior on the other. If you offend another, you are accountable for that and owe it to them to make amends. Let's say someone is giving you the silent treatment and obviously ignoring you. You let them know that you are feeling hurt about their behavior towards you, and then they respond by telling you that you've created your own reality.

It's important to clearly make distinctions here. If a person is in the act of offending or abusing someone physically, sexually, mentally, emotionally or spiritually, *they* are responsible for that.

### Spiritual boundaries

Spiritual boundaries are present when you intimately know yourself, meaning you know what you believe, think, feel, and value. You are comfortable sharing your inner world with others and listening to others share their reality with you. If you differ from another, you become curious, rather than threatened.

You can ask people to guide and assist you to develop your belief system, however, you have the right to choose what to believe in and, ultimately, only you know the spiritual path that is right for you.

Doing all of the exercises in this book will automatically give you spiritual boundaries.

CHAPTER 5: CREATING INTIMACY

## EXERCISE 17: INTIMACY-BUILDING QUESTIONS FOR ROMANTIC RELATIONSHIPS

The following questions are great to answer and share with a partner to enhance intimacy. If you are not currently in a relationship, they'll help you to know yourself better and clarify the ways you would like to relate in an intimate relationship. 'Intimacy Building Questions' is great preparation for the next exercise, 'Creating an Intimate Relationship'.

1. Why are we in this relationship in the first place?

   _____
   _____

2. What will be the early warning signs that our relationship is in trouble?

   _____
   _____

3. What activities and common interests can we develop that will bring us closer together?

   _____
   _____

4. What are we willing to do that we haven't been willing to do with any previous relationship?

   _____
   _____

5. How much space/time do we need apart during the day? Week? Month? Year?

   _____
   _____

6. Ask each other. What should I never do or say to you, even in anger or frustration?

7. Where will this relationship be five years from now?

8. What's the biggest lesson you can learn from me?

9. What's the biggest lesson I can learn from you?

10. What's our code word to use during a conversation/argument where one of us is getting hurt and a time out is needed?

11. When we first meet after being apart for the day, what are the three things you would like me to do or say in the first several minutes?

12. How much room/license do we have to ask the other person to change?

CHAPTER 5: CREATING INTIMACY

13. What changes do you think I'll need to make in order for you to be really happy?

_____
_____

14. What kind of memories do we want to create together?

_____
_____

15. What kind of non-sexual touch or demonstration best says 'I love you' to you?

_____
_____

16. What are the three parts of your body that you most like touched? How?

_____
_____

17. Where should I NOT touch you? Why?

_____
_____

18. How will you let me know when you need to not be touched for a little while?

_____
_____

19. How will we let each other know what we want sexually?

_____

_____

20. What's the biggest sexual turn-off for you?

_____

_____

21. What do you think I like most in regards to our lovemaking?

_____

_____

22. What aspect of my personality is sexy to you?

_____

_____

23. What are the five things you like most about my body? Why?

_____

_____

24. What do you most want to do after we have had sex?

_____

_____

25. What's the most sacred part of you?

_____

_____

CHAPTER 5: CREATING INTIMACY

## ♡ EXERCISE 18: CREATING AN INTIMATE RELATIONSHIP

This exercise will help you get clear on your feelings, thoughts and behaviors (your reality) regarding issues, interactions, aspects and areas of importance in a particular relationship.

Once you have completed the first part of this exercise you will be able to discern how you filter, translate, project, accept or reject the person you are in a relationship with and how this relationship influences your reality. This is essential in understanding how we teach others to treat us, as well as the impact we make on others.

When drawing this picture, art is not the key. Use your gut-level feelings, thoughts and behaviors to illustrate your relationship in a symbolic manner. Remember to include everything that is of importance to you.

There are three parts to this exercise. For it to be effective, do not read parts two or three until you have actually done part one. You will be illustrating your relationship using the following instructions as a guideline.

The diagrams used in this exercise are taken from Peter and Sally's relationship, who were clients of mine. Sally has two children from a previous marriage who live with Peter and Sally. They have been living together for five years. Diagram 10 is Peter's current reality of his relationship with Sally.

### Part 1

1. Use a large piece of paper such as butchers' paper or an artists pad, and colored markers (the diagrams are not displayed in color). Place a circle in the center of the paper with you and your partner's names in it. In the space around the circle you have just drawn, label other circles to represent the areas of importance in your relationship that have an impact on you. The size of the circles, and the distance from you indicate the strength of the impact that each issue or aspect has on you.

Consider the following: needs, values, wants, desires, money, fear, struggle, intimacy, honesty, social, self-worth, children, amount of time spent together, career, sex, future, family, addictions, personal health, self-care, housework, love, fun or any aspect that is important to you and the relationship.

For example, a very large circle or circles placed close to you indicate a great deal of impact. A small circle, or one on the periphery indicates less of an impact. Alternatively, there may be something large, with a big impact far away, yet moving towards you.

2. Choose another colored marker. Next to the circles place a plus (+) and/or minus (-) to indicate whether the impact is positive or negative. Some circles may have only one symbol and others may have both. The size of the symbol will indicate the strength of the positive or negative influence.

Select a different colored marker. Draw arrows between you and the circles impacting you to indicate whether the influence exerted is expanding or diminishing. If a circle represents an issue that is diminishing in your relationship, then draw the arrow pointing away from you. If a circle represents an issue that is expanding, the arrow would be drawn pointing towards you. Some arrows may point in both directions.

For example, if you have recently experienced a change, or are working on this area in your relationship, the negative influence of this issue is probably diminishing.

Over the page is a diagram symbolizing Peter and Sally's relationship. You may have a completely different scenario - this is one of a million possibilities!

CHAPTER 5: CREATING INTIMACY

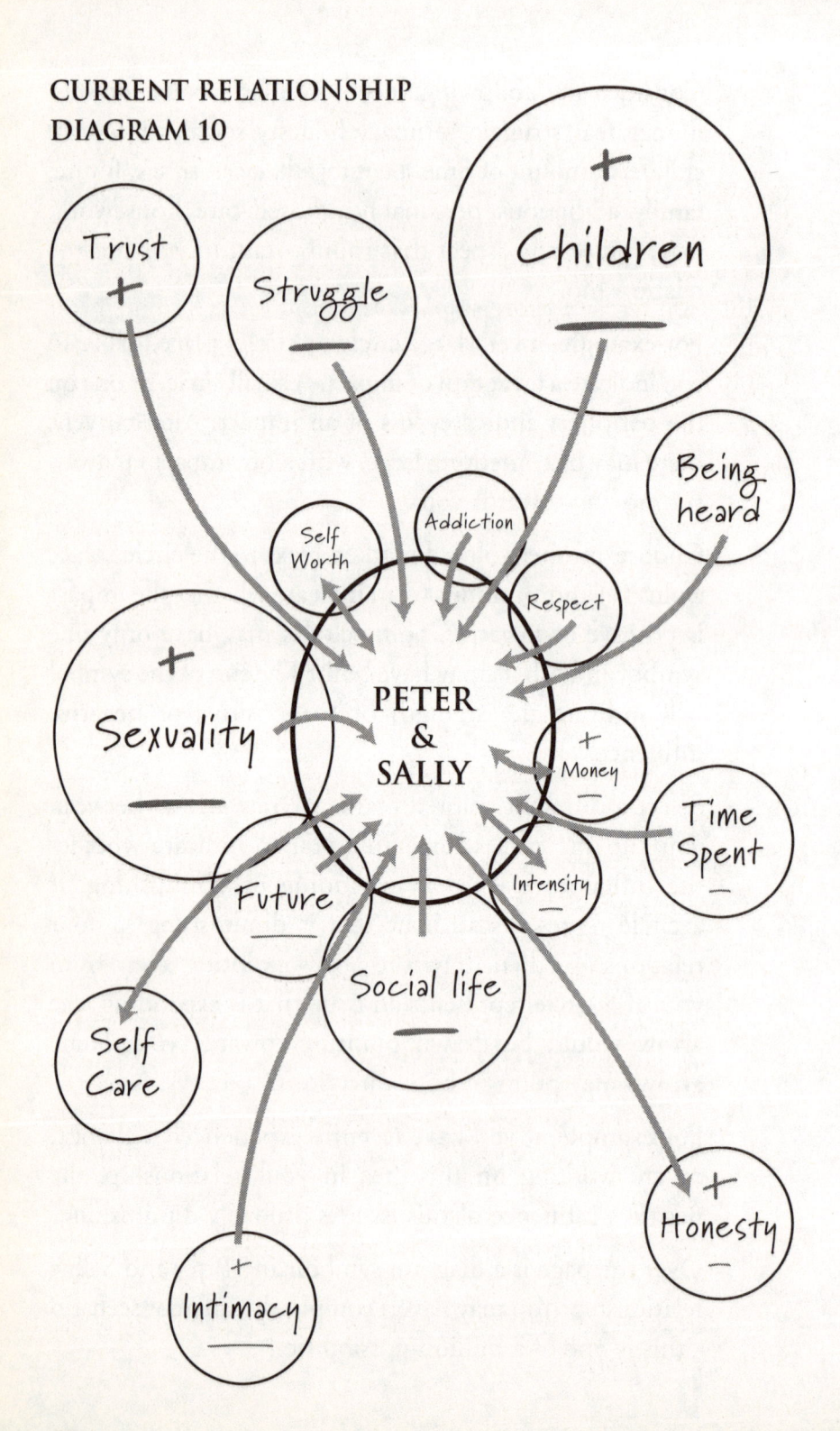

## CURRENT RELATIONSHIP
## DIAGRAM 10

174

## Part 2

Once you have completed the picture of your relationship, the following questions are the second stage of this process. I suggest you find a trusted friend or someone you feel safe to debrief your experience and your responses with. To go deeply into this, you might want to use a professional counselor or coach to help you. This part of the process will give you insight and help you clarify how you would like your relationship to be in the future. Look at your picture and answer the following questions. The responses are an example, taken from Peter.

1. Have you forgotten an issue, aspect or area of importance in your relationship?

    *Yes, I had forgotten love – I have never really known what love is so I have always felt uncomfortable about expressing it and saying that I love Sally. This creates increasing struggle in our relationship.*

2. Look at the arrows you drew. Do the arrows that move toward you stop at the edge of your circle, inside your circle or do they pass through your circle? Considering boundaries, what insights do you get from this?

    *I noticed that my arrows all landed right inside the circle. As though all the issues are attacking and penetrating the relationship. It is really clear to me now that we have no boundaries in the relationship.*

3. How are your arrows shaped? Are they long, short, straight or do they have hooks, curves or kinks in them? Why?

    *The arrows are shaped with curves – either very short or very long. I think this symbolizes 'all or nothing'. The 'curvy' arrows seem to represent the 'slippery' issues that we are not addressing in our relationship (which are all of them!).*

CHAPTER 5: CREATING INTIMACY

4. Use a marker and divide your paper into four quarters. How are your circles grouped? Are certain types of impacting circles located in one quadrant more than the others? Are the circles too close together or spread out? Do you have enough space regarding your issues, or are you isolated from your issues (too much space). See Diagram 11.

    *The circles are spread evenly throughout each quadrant. The most significant quarter I noticed was the top right one. The circle for 'children' dominated nearly one whole quarter. I also noticed how addiction, lack of respect, and lack of being heard are in the same quadrant. These issues are 'blocking' Sally and I from creating healthy relationships with the children.*

5. Are any of the circles bigger than your relationship? What does this mean to you?

    *Yes, sexuality and children are bigger issues.*

6. Determine how this relationship looks, feels and sounds to you right now.

    *This relationship scenario feels overwhelming, engulfing and looks chaotic to me. It seems 'noisy' and unbalanced.*

7. What are you learning from this relationship and how is this making you a better person?

    *I am learning how important it is to set boundaries, so that I feel less overwhelmed and engulfed. By setting limits and addressing the core issues such as sexuality, addiction and intensity, I can be more available in my relationship with Sally and the children.*

8. Does your relationship have a purpose and intention? If so, what is it?

    *No, we had never really considered what we wanted to*

give and take from the relationship. This has come as a big surprise.

9. What do you give to the relationship and what do you take from it?

To be honest – I feel like it's all take. I feel resentful about giving to the relationship when I feel overwhelmed by the negative impact that certain issues are having on me – such as how to spend time with Sally and not only the children. I am beginning to understand how important it is to give to the relationship, for example, my time, and to actively work on improving my connection with Sally.

10. What specific changes do you feel you could begin to implement right now?

Have a weekly family meeting where everyone can discuss their needs and wants and plan on how they will get them met. For example, Sally and I will have a date once a fortnight. This will be non-negotiable – so we meet our need to stay connected, create more intimacy and have more fun by spending time together without the children.

CHAPTER 5: CREATING INTIMACY

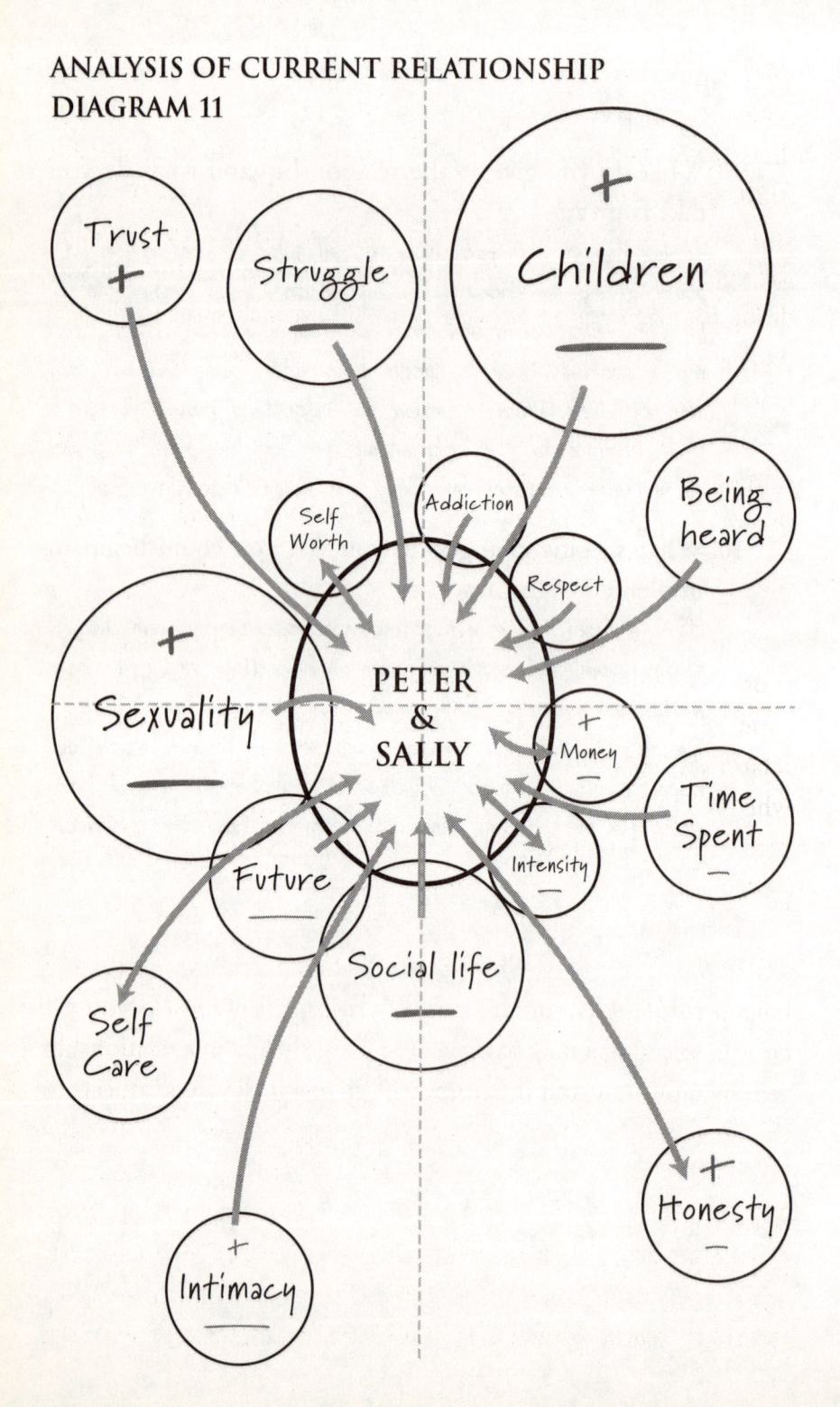

## ANALYSIS OF CURRENT RELATIONSHIP
## DIAGRAM 11

- Trust +
- Struggle −
- Children +  −
- Self Worth
- Addiction
- Being heard
- Respect
- Sexuality +  −
- PETER & SALLY
- Money +  −
- Time Spent −
- Future −
- Intensity
- Self Care
- Social life −
- Intimacy +  −
- Honesty +  −

178

## Part 3

Take a clean sheet of paper and do the exercise again, this time drawing your relationship the way you want it to be. It's preferable to do this drawing with your current partner. If you are single, you can draw this to intentionally create an intimate relationship for your future. If you are currently in a relationship and are doing the drawing on your own, then you may want to share it with your partner when you are finished. This is a great way to foster intimacy.

To begin this exercise, I recommend that you decide on the purpose and intention of your relationship. You might think this is obvious (e.g. to get married, raise a family and grow old together). Yet, what I've discovered is that couples who get clear on the purpose and intention of their relationship and write it down, keep their relationships on track and they seem to be more satisfied than those who don't. Plus, the purpose and intention can change over time as your circumstances change. Intentionally creating your relationship gives you more control and better success than when you don't. When doing this, you are actually making a commitment, aligning your energy and creating a structure for more spontaneity.

It doesn't matter if you write this with your partner or by yourself, as long as you both agree that each of you is allowed to have it fulfilled. If you are single, writing this will help you get clear in selecting a new partner. If you are already in a relationship writing a purpose and intention will help you eliminate aspects of the relationship that cause chaos and conflict. Before I met my husband I wrote out my purpose and intention for a relationship. My purpose was to experience intimacy, deep love and to evolve spiritually. My intention was for the relationship to furnish me with companionship in the form of a playmate and someone to travel the world with. I also wanted to have great sex within a

CHAPTER 5: CREATING INTIMACY

monogamous relationship, to eventually be married and grow old together. I didn't want to be with someone who had young children or children who would live with us (this was because I had previously married very young and already raised a family). Here are some examples of couples' purpose and intentions for their relationship.

Peter and Sally: The purpose of their relationship is to have fun, be interdependent and experience synergy as a family. Their intention is to be actively involved in sports and family activities, have the freedom to do things separately and to be involved as a family in their church.

Matt and Anna: The purpose of their relationship is to support each other to be all that they can be and to create things together. Their intention is to design and build a home, have children, enjoy fulfilling work and to create an environment that fosters creativity, wealth and harmony.

When creating your new relationship, it is important to include your personal needs, and shared values, wants and desires. Once you've finished, make sure to share your new picture with your partner or if you are single, with a trusted friend, a professional counselor or coach.

Good luck and may the force be with you!

Diagram 12 from Part 3 shows a picture of the relationship Peter and Sally committed to create. Peter and Sally drew the picture together.

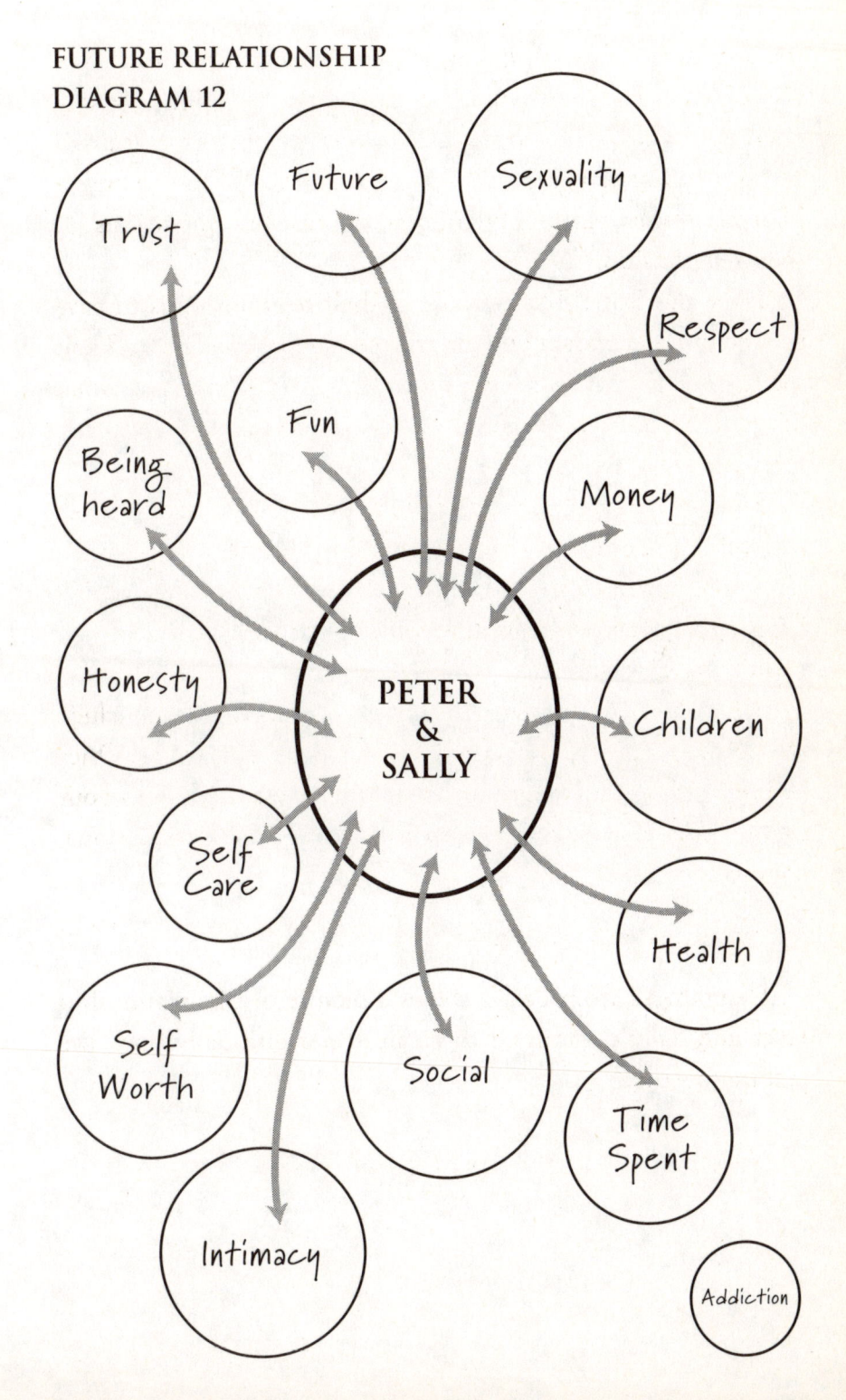

SET YOURSELF FREE IN RELATIONSHIPS

**FUTURE RELATIONSHIP
DIAGRAM 12**

- Trust
- Future
- Sexuality
- Respect
- Being heard
- Fun
- Money
- Honesty
- PETER & SALLY
- Children
- Self Care
- Health
- Self Worth
- Social
- Time Spent
- Intimacy
- Addiction

# CHAPTER 5: CREATING INTIMACY

# EPILOGUE

# THE LAST DANCE

I spent the night in my father's hospital room the night before we made the decision to take him off life support. He was restless, slipping in and out of consciousness, calling out "help - help" every hour or so. Before I asked the nurse for some sedation to make him comfortable, I got as close to him as the tubes and apparatuses would allow. Stroking his forehead and whispering in his ear I told him a story - the story of his life.

> *Once upon a time a special little boy named Johnny was born. Johnny had three older sisters and a beloved dog named "Major", who was his best friend. Johnny was a good boy, giving all the money he earned from his paper route to his widowed mother, which helped to feed the family. Known to ride as 'fast as the wind', Johnny regularly escaped from his house full of women, racing on his bicycle with Major alongside.*
>
> *When he grew up he met his princess, Laura at a ball. They married just after Johnny was drafted in the Army Air Corps to fight in World War II. (I sang 'their' song to him even better than The Andrew Sisters - "Don't Sit Under the Apple Tree With Anyone Else But Me").*

*Having two beautiful daughters, John still lived surrounded by women. His second daughter, Shirley was supposed to be the boy, but John didn't care because he loved his girls and was very protective of them. John was a good provider for his family, working two jobs to buy them a house and he took them on a family vacation every year.*

*John liked to be active. He played golf, belonged to a scuba diving club and even built his own boat! He took his youngest daughter, Shirley, on that boat sharing many adventures dancing across the ocean, as well as deep under the water. He once told her that when he was under the water he could forget about all of his worries and just let go. He loved being under the water. A satisfied hunter, John was very proud of the fact that he kept his family in a bounty of lobster, abalone and deep sea bass. John loved camping and the outdoors and when he got older he loved to go fishing, filling his freezer with trout.*

*John danced with his daughters at their weddings - more than once! The last time he shared the dance floor with Shirley was at his 50th Golden Wedding Anniversary Party - the greatest surprise his daughters ever pulled off. That night there were many good dances, just like back at Alpine Village with the "Beer Barrel Polka".*

*One day, John got really tired. He was tired of dancing with Laura and even tired of TV. On Valentine's Day he decided to stop dancing and went to the hospital. For a while, he was surrounded in darkness and fear as the tubes and needles kept him imprisoned. Finally, his family gathered around him to help him find the light and told him it was ok to let go.*

*Again I whispered in my Dad's ear, "you have been*

> *the best Father you could be and I have learned so much from you. You taught me to take care of myself and you taught me how to dance. I love you Daddy, it's ok to let go now and go to the light', I whispered tenderly.* "Go and find Mama and Pop, Auntie Millie and Auntie Olga. They are waiting for you. And when it's my time to go to the light, I will be looking for you - and I know you'll to be there with your arms wide open, waiting to show me the way."

That night my Father slept peacefully and I felt peaceful with the decision to let him go and stop his suffering. The next morning, along with the minister our family made a circle around his bed and prayed for God's love to fill us all and for God's will to be done. We then told the doctor to take off all life support and make my father comfortable.

After the decision, fear hit me in the guts. Doubt crept in and I confided in my husband, Eric, that I was afraid we might be killing my Father. My Mother and sister didn't want to be in the room when they took off the life support, so they stayed in the corridor as Eric and I stood on each side of my Dad, holding his hand. With a fear-filled heart I started to pray and when I was finished, I whispered in my Dad's ear, "Daddy I promised you I wouldn't let you suffer. We are taking those horrible tubes out of you now. We are setting you free." I watched my Father closely as they took the needles from his arms and the painful feeding tube from his nose.

You know, God answers prayer. When they pulled the painful feeding tube out of his nose, my Dad opened his eyes and locked on to mine. It was then I knew that he had heard me all along. I'm sure he mustered up all his strength when he said out loud, "thank you". Those were his last words as he slipped into a coma. I replied, "thank you God".

## EPILOGUE: THE LAST DANCE

Somewhat later, after my Mom and Dads "T.V time" my sister took my mother home. They couldn't be with him when he died. Too much fear, bad feelings and not knowing what to do. It was just too much for them. Eric and I stayed with him for the last dance.

Death is as beautiful as birth. Eric and I felt privileged and grateful to be of service to my father. His passing was one of the most intimate and beautiful experiences that we have shared. When my father took his last breath, we completely connected with him, holding him, ushering him to the light and saying the Lords Prayer. Because I had resolved my unfinished family business, I could be totally present and intimate with my father, helping him make his transition in a peaceful and loving way. It was our last dance, and it was wonderful beyond words.

Witnessing my Fathers life and death gave me the most profound gift. A reminder that if my husband and I didn't continue to set intentions and stay actively accountable, creating the relationship we desire, we could easily end up dancing like my parents did. And that is not our dance.

Later that night when Eric and I finally went to bed, we lay awake for a long time staring into each other's eyes. There are so many opportunities to share profound experiences with another if you're prepared to be present. My dear Dad had brought us closer. Before we went to sleep, we promised each other we'd do whatever it takes to stay connected, create intimacy and evolve spiritually.

Thank you Daddy for letting me witness your life. For showing me how you dance and for letting me dance my own dance.

# BIBLIOGRAPHY & SUGGESTED READING

*Alcoholics Anonymous,* The Big Book. Third Edition.
New York: Alcoholics Anonymous World Services Inc., 1976.

Bradshaw, John. *Bradshaw On: The Family: A Revolutionary Way Of Self Discovery.*
Pompano Beach Fl.: Health Communications, 1988.

Carnes, Patrick. *Out Of The Shadows: Understanding Sexual Addiction.* Minneapolis, Mn.: CompCare, 1983.

Carnes, Patrick. *Don't call it love: Recovery from Sexual Addiction.* USA: Bantam Books, 1992.

Firestone, Robert W. *The Fantasy Bond: Effects Of Psychological Defenses On Interpersonal Relations.*
New York: Human Sciences Press, Inc., 1987.

Firestone, Robert W. *The Fantasy Bond: Effects Of Psychological Defenses On Interpersonal Relations.*
New York: Human Sciences Press, Inc., 1987.

Firestone, Robert W; Catlett, Joyce. *Fear of Intimacy.*
New York: American Psychological Association (APA); 4th edition (December, 2000).

# BIBLIOGRAPHY AND SUGGESTED READING

Gibran, Kahil. *The Prophet.* New York: Random House, 1951.

Mellody, Pia. *Facing Love Addiction: Giving yourself the Power to Change the Way You Love.*
Australia: Harper Collins Publishers, 1992.

Miller, Alice. *The Drama Of The Gifted Child.*
New York: Basic Books, Inc., 1981.

Norwood, Robin. *Women Who Love Too Much.* Los Angeles: Jeremy Tarcher, Inc., 1985.

Schaef, Anne Wilson. *Escape From Intimacy: Untangling the "Love" Addictions: Sex, Romance, Relationships.*
San Francisco: Harper and Row, 1989.

*Sex and Love Addicts Anonymous.*
Boston: The Augustine Fellowship, Sex and Love Addicts Anonymous, Fellowship-Wide Services, Inc.,1986.

*The Twelve Steps For Adult Children Of Alcoholics And Other Dysfunctional Families.*
San Diego: Recovery Publications, 1987.

Wegscheider-Cruse, Sharon. *Choice-Making.*
Pompano Beach, Fl.: Health Communications, 1985.

# Resources from Shirley Smith

For more information visit our websites:
www.SetYourselfFree.com.au or www.theradiantgroup.com.au
Call: +61 2 9953 7000
Email: info@SetYourselfFree.com.au

## BOOKS BY SHIRLEY SMITH

### SET YOURSELF FREE: ANNIVERSARY EDITION
*Break the cycle of co-dependency and compulsive addictive behavior.*

ISBN: 9780975102107
Pub:   The Radiant Group Pty Ltd

**Australia's #1 selling title on co-dependency.**
This new edition includes real life, inspiring, Australian stories from those who set themselves free! The book is more relevant today than when first written over a decade ago. Why? Because co-dependency and addictive behavior is a costly and pervasive element of Australian society; increasing significantly since the book was originally released.

*A must read for people with addictive personalities ...... and those who love them!*

### SET YOURSELF FREE IN RELATIONSHIPS
*Essential skills to teach others how to treat you.*

ISBN: 0977276007
Pub:   Artisan Educational Systems LLC.

Unhealthy relationships are becoming the 'rule' rather than the exception in people's lives. These relationships damage self-confidence and leave people with feelings of depression, frustration, anxiety and despair. Shirley says: "What most people don't realize is that we teach others how to treat us" This book delivers essential skills to create happy, healthy and intimate relationships. Shirley Smith shows the reader how to learn to love others while honoring their true selves.

### GAME OF LIFE PLAYBOOK
*Currently out of print.*
ISBN: 9781863590914
Pub:   Bantam Books

*This book shows you how to enjoy playing the game of life - and how to win!*

**ORDER NOW**

**ATTENTION** Health Care Professionals and Practitioners
If you would like to have the *Set Yourself Free Series* - books and audio programs available to sell to your client base please call +61 2 9953 7000 or email info@setyourselffree.com.au

We will send you details of our wholesale rates and quantity discounts.

# AUDIO PROGRAMS
## BY SHIRLEY SMITH

All Audio Programs are available on CD or downloadable. Check the website for prices and special package savings. Shipment is available worldwide.

**FREE CD**

### THE IMPORTANCE OF A STRONG PERSONAL FOUNDATION
*Duration: 61 min.*
*Free Audio Program available on CD or downloadable from our website.*

Many people ask us what our *Set Yourself Free* Program involves and what it takes to see positive change and results in their lives. If you would like to receive a complimentary audio program, explaining in depth what's required to build a strong personal foundation and an overview of this process, then please log online to receive a complimentary copy: http://www.SetYourselfFree.com.au - check under 'Free Resources'. We will post it to you wherever you are or you can download the lecture.

Alternatively send us an email with your name, contact number and address to info@SetYourelfFree.com.au.

You may find that listening to this very informative lecture by Shirley Smith will help you identify the areas in your life that you would like to change. If you find this audio program useful, please pass it on to a friend or family member.

## THE SET YOURSELF FREE SERIES

### BREAKING THE FAMILY TRANCE
*Single CD: 61 min.*

History doesn't have to repeat itself! This audio program will help you unlock unconscious psychological defenses that keep you stuck. These defenses create destructive habits and sabotaging behaviors causing you to recycle the same unfulfilling relationships and circumstances.

### SET YOURSELF FREE FROM ADDICTIVE BEHAVIOURS
*Single CD: Duration 63 min.*

This program teaches the critical distinction between compulsive and addictive behavior and why the approach to their treatment must be different. You will learn a simple, 3-Step model to treat the 'process addictions' to: work, sex, money (gambling, spending, debting) relationships, raging, rushing, religion, romance, eating, starving, body image, internet, sport or being busy. Learn to have more consistency in your daily life.

This program is a must for people caught in addictive behaviors... and for those who care about them!

### CO-DEPENDENCY RELATIONSHIPS AND YOU
*Single CD: 62 min.*

This program explains what's required to establish a solid, soulful relationship with yourself first, and then shows you how to expand to form healthy relationships with others. This process is possible whether you are currently in a relationship or not. If you want to learn to make choices that satisfy you and changes that last, then you can't afford not to hear this comprehensive presentation on Co-dependency, Relationships and You!

## THE RELATIONSHIPS SERIES

### THE ROMANCE TRANCE
*Double CD Pack: 83 min.*

Learn to stop power struggling and discover how to relate between the paradoxes that are present in all relationships. Gain deeper insights into your patterns of relating, receive guidance and encouragement to express yourself honestly and discover the tools to create healthy, loving relationships built on a spiritual foundation of hope.

### IS IT INTIMACY OR IS IT INTENSITY?
*Single CD: 52 min.*

Do you swing between highs and lows, causing you to seesaw between intense pleasure and intense pain? This highly informative audio program gives you deep insights into the nature of intimacy and how we use intensity as an addictive substitute. Lack of real intimacy is the source of pain, confusion, loneliness and mistrust in relationships. Discover the true characteristics of intimacy, why it is fundamental to your happiness and how to create it in your relationships today.

### THE CO-ADDICTIVE LOVE DANCE
*Single CD: 39 min.*

This CD is not only reserved for romantic lovers. Many mothers and daughters; mothers and sons; fathers and daughters; fathers and sons... or in fact any two people can dance this dance! Co-addictive relationships are set up from unresolved issues from our formative years. These include neglect, abandonment, abuse, engulfment, extreme control and unmet needs. 'The dance' distracts partners from discovering their real issues, so they don't have to acknowledge the emptiness and loneliness in their relationship or their unresolved childhood wounds.

They are caught in an addictive cycle (a swirling dance) that is an intense replacement for true intimacy and real relating.

If you want to stop dancing and create honest, loving, 'real relationships' ... then this program is for you!

---

Audio programs available from:
www.SetYourselfFree.com.au or www.theradiantgroup.com.au

# PROGRAMS & SERVICES

## SET YOURSELF FREE PROGRAM

Presented by Shirley Smith, and her team of trained facilitators, *The Set Yourself Free* program is highly pro-active and provides a unique structure of support to move you quickly, thoroughly and easily through the process of transformation. You will gain more confidence and choice, providing a greater sense of security, freedom, purpose, competency and connection in your life - and you will see significant results much sooner than you think!

*Set Yourself Free Programs* includes a 3-day intensive plus an 8-week extension personal foundation program. The extension program supports you to integrate and expand upon the changes you make at the 3-day intensive. It includes a workbook, lectures and one-hour individual assessments with your facilitator to monitor your progress.

The extension program is offered in a group, face-to-face format, via tele-classes and soon via video-conferencing.

Each 8-week module covers a separate topic. These topics include:
- Breaking the Family Trance
- Setting Yourself Free in Relationships
- Set Yourself Free from Self-Sabotage
- Overcoming the Fear of Success
- Sexuality, Sensuality, Spirituality and Shame

Other programs include: Creating Intimacy- intensive residential for couples, co-facilitated by Shirley Smith and Eric Rose (see following pages).

If you're ready to move away from frustrating, repetitive and painful circumstances and you are ready to move forward and step into your greatness then we invite you to Set Yourself Free!

"The Set Yourself Free Program is certainly a challenging experience and one of the best 3 day intensives I've ever had. The weekend helped me come to terms with my fears and start to face them, alongside a rock solid realization that none of us is alone in our worries and feelings of inadequacy, so we never have to be alone again. This exciting journey of self - discovery is only just beginning..." - Mark Kennedy, Radio Announcer

### LOW COST 1.5 HOUR ASSESSMENT SESSIONS

We offer a 1.5-hour assessment session with a facilitator trained by Shirley Smith. This is available face-to-face in our office in Sydney, Australia; over the phone worldwide, and soon to be available via video conferencing. The process involves answering an 8-page questionnaire written by Shirley Smith and debriefing your responses with your facilitator.

The purpose of these sessions is to help you get clear on your situation and to assist you to discover the support that is right for you. It may be services we offer at The Radiant Group or we may refer you to services and practitioners outside of our organization. Contact us on info@SetYourselfFree.com.au

# PROGRAMS & SERVICES

## EMPOWERING COMMUNICATIONS

Consider the world's most successful and influential people and you will discover they have all mastered the same skill - effective communication!

Without well-developed communication skills you are limiting your ability to achieve your desired outcomes. Being able to clearly present your ideas and objectives, understanding when and how to be assertive and knowing how to handle difficult people is fundamental to your success in any social or business environment.

Presented by Shirley Smith, *Empowering Communications* teaches breakthrough skills that are essential to become a compelling and masterful communicator. Shirley is exceptional at eliciting your authentic self-expression. Over and over again our graduates say to us that the *Empowering Communications Program* has been the most life-changing and confidence building work they have ever done. This program is Shirley's "signature piece" and many say her best work.

By the end of the *Empowering Communications Program* you will have even more confidence and conviction to strive for any outcome you wish for in life!

*'If you are wanting to tap into your creativity, lead & influence, amplify your confidence, be a MEMORABLE communicator, stretch your comfort zone, experience accelerated learning, surrender to fun and humor, discover the chemistry of effective communication or just walk your talk, then give yourself permission to participate in Empowering Communications'*

— David McGuinness, partner Blake Dawson Waldron Lawyers.

## EMPOWERING COMMUNICATIONS GRADUATE COACHING PROGRAM

In conjunction with the *Empowering Communications Program (ECP)*, graduates who have previously attended ECP are invited to return as a coach for the current participants. This is an accelerated program and allows you to integrate the ECP skills you have learned at a new level. Shirley says: *"when you teach what you need to learn it locks the skills into your neurology and becomes a natural part of your behavior."* Being a coach will stretch you and bring you the greatest rewards. This is a chance to work closely with Shirley where you will be given every opportunity to learn what it takes to coach and facilitate with excellence.

# PROGRAMS & SERVICES

## COACHES & CONSULTING

Coaching helps you to design any aspect of your life, or in fact your entire life, the way you truly want it to be. The coaching process lets you expand and strengthen **Who** you are, get clear about **What** you want, and develop strategies on **How** to achieve it.

Most people have unconscious beliefs that "hard work and doing it on your own" creates happiness, wealth and success in life. Often the price people pay for success is poor health, lessened productivity, not having enough time to enjoy life and strained family relationships.

Coaching is a collaborative process built upon a synergistic relationship between coach and client. Having a coach is like having a personal trainer for your relationships and personal life. Regarding your professional life, having a coach is like having a business partner without sharing the profits of your growth!

Anyone, from any walk of life, who wants to be, do, have and express more in their professional and/or personal lives, will benefit from a coaching relationship. Coaching also works brilliantly for anyone feeling stuck, stifled or stagnant in any way and is ready for a breakthrough.

### COACHES: Shirley Smith

In relationships and organizations, personally and professionally, Shirley is a talented trouble-shooter and especially good at using all the resources at hand to get the desired outcomes. In addition to assisting those who feel blocked or are in a time of transition and wish to move forward in their lives, Shirley also coaches executives, professionals and managers in business. With twenty years experience in the field of coaching and personal development, Shirley expertly consults small business and the corporate sector, helping executives understand the underlying issues that sabotage an organization's success.

Shirley custom designs programs to meet the needs of your organization. Training is available on Communication, Sales, Leadership, Team Building, and Culture Change. She is available for coaching consultations by phone and soon via video conferencing.

For further information or to make an enquiry please contact contact us by email on info@shirleysmith.com or visit www.shirleysmith.com

# PROGRAMS & SERVICES

## COACHES: Eric Rose

Eric Rose is a certified coach, facilitator with the Radiant Group and a Myers Briggs Practitioner, which uses Jung's theory of psychological types.

Eric works at a deep intuitive level with both men and women, around relationship and life transition issues. He uses Emotional Freedom Technique and Relationship Energy Re-patterning, which is an introduction into the body's electrical system, using meridian points to facilitate deep and lasting change around trauma and destructive, negative belief patterns.

Eric and Shirley are married and have been partners for ten years. They often work together with couples and families who want healing and intimacy in their relationships. Eric has two grown sons and lives in Sydney's North Shore and the Blue Mountains with Shirley and their little dog Sassy.

For further information visit www.theradiantgroup.com.au or email Eric Rose: eric@theradiantgroup.com.au